Frederic Cushman Newhall

With General Sheridan in Lee's Last Campaign

Frederic Cushman Newhall

With General Sheridan in Lee's Last Campaign

ISBN/EAN: 9783337813871

Printed in Europe, USA, Canada, Australia, Japan

Cover: Foto ©ninafisch / pixelio.de

More available books at **www.hansebooks.com**

WITH GENERAL SHERIDAN

IN

LEE'S LAST CAMPAIGN.

BY

A STAFF OFFICER.

PHILADELPHIA:
J. B. LIPPINCOTT & CO.
1866.

Entered, according to Act of Congress, in the year 1866, by

J. B. LIPPINCOTT & CO.,

In the Clerk's Office of the District Court of the United States for the Eastern District of Pennsylvania.

*" Whoe'er amidst the sons
Of reason, valour, liberty, and virtue,
Displays distinguished merit, is a noble
Of Nature's own creating."*

---

*" Till we called
Both Field and City ours, he never stood
To ease his breast with panting."*

PREFACE.

As it is perfectly true, it seems proper to say that this slight sketch has not in any way been prompted by General Sheridan, who will be aware of its contents for the first time when he closes this book. He has not even been afforded the opportunity to speak for himself, which might perhaps with politeness have been tendered, and therefore he is not behind any of the scenes.

If from want of him the story has lost interest in the telling, doubtless it will be conceded that it has gained in propriety, as public self-eulogy and self-defense have of late grown somewhat unpopular.

The sketch, such as it is, has no object in the world but to fairly present the general and his campaigning to such readers as the book shall find; and the writer refrains from announcing himself only because of a conviction that, if the famous names now upon the title-page fail to receive attention, it would avail very little to add his own; he does not wish to avoid the responsibility of a narrative which of necessity makes mention of many gallant officers of our army, and if any whose name appears on these pages care to learn the source of this small tributary to the ocean of our war history, he can trace it by an inquiry of General Sheridan or the publishers, if he happen to have no friend possessed of the weighty secret.

PHILADELPHIA, *October 1st*, 1866.

CONTENTS.

CHAPTER I.
Major-General P. H. Sheridan.................................. 9

CHAPTER II.
From the Shenandoah to the James...................... 28

CHAPTER III.
Sheridan's Cavalry.. 37

CHAPTER IV.
Feeling Lee's Right Flank....................................... 49

CHAPTER V.
A Fight about Five Forks....................................... 81

CHAPTER VI.
Lee breaks Cover... 127

CHAPTER VII.
The Pursuit.. 134

CHAPTER VIII.
The Ninth of April, Sixty-five............................... 207

CHAPTER IX.
Breaking Ranks... 225

CHAPTER I.

MAJOR-GENERAL P. H. SHERIDAN.

Very few civilians of the North would know General Sheridan should they see him. After graduating at West Point he was almost constantly on duty in the far West, and if ever before the war he came to the Atlantic coast, he was unknown to fame, and attracted no attention. During the rebellion he was seldom out of the field; and as soon as Johnston's army surrendered, without waiting for the grand review at Washington, which would have so delightfully introduced him to many loyal people, he hurried off to the Department of the Gulf to take command of the troops concentrating there for the expected campaign in Texas against Kirby Smith, who had presented an extremely defiant front so long as he was in no danger of being properly looked after.

As is well known, the general has remained in command of that department, now called the Military Division of the Gulf, with his headquarters in New Orleans; and thus, except in his hurried trip from Washington to St. Louis, on his way to Texas, has had no opportunity to meet those who most appreciate his services and whom he most regards. It is thought, therefore, that in this familiar narrative of his operations in the last campaign against Lee, the reader will be glad to find something concerning General Sheridan himself as a soldier and as a man, and will be glad to feel on rather better terms with the general than he has ever been before, especially if, as is likely, he has known him only through his very bad photographs and the stories of his very bad swearing.

But no attempt will be made here to write his "life," or to follow him through his boyhood and early manhood to the days of his military distinction, though we may mention that it has already been printed of the general that he was born in Massachusetts and in Ohio; that his father was wealthy and a prominent politician; and that his parents, while strictly honest, were extremely poor, and that he contributed to their support by driving a water-cart through the dusty streets of his native town.

The reader can take his choice of these beginnings, for no importance is attached to either of the stories, as they are not necessary to this sketch, and are useless in a general way, inasmuch as man's intellect is not in any walk of life always in exact proportion to his birth.

It will suffice to speak here of him and of his characteristics as we find them when he was already distinguished as a soldier. It is the purpose of this narration to avoid idealizing General Sheridan, endowing him with virtues which he does not possess, and clothing him with a garb that he does not pretend to wear; but as it is considered the merest justice to give his due to a most notorious sinner, a much less intending one may claim as much. To borrow, then, an injunction made in another connection: "Let us be thankful that we have a good general, but don't let us lie about him;" let us kiss the Book and give our testimony to the best of our knowledge and belief, especially as it has been said that truth is always amusing.

There is a popular idea current that the general is only congenial with the roughest phases of war and military life, and an erroneous impression has been formed by many that he is an exceedingly profane man. Mr. Buchanan Read has ascribed to him "a terrible oath," and a writer in *Harper's Magazine* last summer fathered upon him some terrific imprecations, and led the public to think that the general's tongue is a mint where strange oaths are coined of most unique and awful pattern. It grieved many simple people that his good record should be tarnished by such evil practices, and some curious letters found their way to his headquarters, principally from motherly women no doubt, remonstrating kindly with him on this account, and begging him to abandon this vicious habit, if only for the sake of example, to say nothing of his immortal soul. If this evil report was true, of course they did right to so remonstrate; but it was not. Everybody has heard that in the army the amenities of home-life are not much regarded, and it is pretty well known that there the adjectives of the schools are dropped, and oaths are taken up when substantives are to be qualified. On the march they are as common as footfalls, so common everywhere in talk that to give force to language on such supreme occasions as often arise, the strongest adjective would be simply ridiculous, and would fall upon the soldier's ear with no more impression than the falling leaf. It is proper to believe that in times of trial on hard-fought fields a good example is the best address to the rank and file, but there are moments when men are blinded by confusion and panic, and have no eyes to see anything but the overwhelming peril, and to look for means of escape. Then they must be spoken to—not in words of calm remonstrance, but in fiery words that claim attention; then, perhaps, some lusty oaths will gain a hearing, buffet back the panic and retrieve disorder, and on such occasions the general has been heard to swear freely, not fearful oaths of elaborate design, but everyday, common curses, that are always on the ear among these men, and come most readily to the lips when swearing must be done. So much is true of him as it is of almost every officer who leads his troops into battle; but it is hoped that the false impression in regard to his habitual profanity may be dispelled at the outset, for perhaps the reader has been thinking him little better than a ruffian, "a very good soldier no doubt, but not the man for decent society and that sort of thing, you know," as perhaps he said to himself or his wife as he read of the oaths of curious device.

The general is short in stature—below the medium—with nothing superfluous about him, square-shouldered, muscular, wiry to the last degree, and as nearly insensible to hardship and fatigue as is consistent with humanity. He has a strangely-shaped head, with a large bump of something or other—combativeness probably—behind the ears, which inconveniences him almost as much as it does his enemies in the field, for there being no general demand for hats that would fit him, the general never has one that will stay on his head. This leads him to take his hat in his hand very often; that action probably suggests cheering something on, and, a fight being in progress and troops needing encouragement, by a simple sequence he usually finds himself among them, where he risks the valuable life of the commanding general, not to mention casualties to staff officers.

His face is very much tanned by exposure, but is lighted up by uncommonly keen eyes, which would stamp him anywhere as a man of quickness and force, while its whole character would betray him to be a soldier, with its firm chin, high cheek bones, and crisp moustache.

He is exacting on duty and hard on delinquents, and his ideas of duty are peculiar, as evinced by the fact that he has never issued orders of encouragement or congratulation to his troops before or after campaigns or battles. He has apparently taken it for granted that all under his command would do as well as they could, and that they did so quite as a matter of course. And to this soldierly view the troops always responded. Understanding so well what they were fighting for and the issues at stake, they would not fight harder to accomplish results simply for the satisfaction of having them recounted. It is not intended, however, to criticise the action of those commanding officers who have done differently in this matter, for no troops did better than those whose deeds have been so recounted, and certainly they did no worse for the encouraging words published among them on the eve of battle.

This trait is alluded to only as an indication of the general's habit of action and thought. But the facts will refute what a writer said in a Boston newspaper last spring, that "the cavalry was fortunate in carrying the trumpet," or words to that effect. A most unworthy slur, for although since the days of Cæsar few generals have been better entitled to indite triumphant orders and dispatches than was General Sheridan at the end of the last campaign, he refrained from both, and went off to a new department without ever so much as a word of farewell or praise to his gallant cavalry. If, with Lee's flag of truce in his hand, he had turned in his saddle and wound a merry blast of triumph to his troops, history would pardon him the egotism, which could have offended none but those whose sense of propriety was sharpened by envy and malice, and that uncharitableness from which we ask to be delivered. And doubtless the loyal people, watching the war during the first weary years, would have welcomed the wildest hyperbole announcing such real and material results as his operations brought about, under Providence, in this last campaign.

It should be remembered, too, that it is much easier to be cold and dignified on paper under the depressing influences of disaster than in the jubilant moments of success. When General Sheridan wrote that General Early was "whirling up the valley," perhaps the expression was a strong one to apply to so solid a body as an army; but it is safe to conclude that if General Sheridan's army had been whirling *down* the valley, the greatest stickler for dignity could not have complained of the tone of his dispatches apprising the Government of the unhappy fact. Generals are human, and their dispatches catch their tone from the surroundings. Eager words from the battle-field only echo the sounds on the writer's ear: officers congratulating warmly, and troops cheering madly; and if this is borne in mind, General Sheridan has proved himself in the midst of many successes to be an eminently modest man.

He is self-reliant enough but not vain-glorious; shuns notoriety, and is abashed before the popular applause, although aware of the services he has been able to render the country; accords all due praise to his associates, but is tenacious of his rights if suspecting any attempt at their invasion.

Being rather reserved, he does not care much for general society, but when comfortably established in headquarters, is hospitable, lives well, and likes to have congenial guests drop in upon his mess. He seems to care most for the company of the placid and easy-going, and is fond of a quiet chat about old times on the frontier with such boon companions as General D. McM. Gregg of the cavalry, General Geo. Crook of the Army of West Virginia, and the gallant General David Russell of the Sixth Corps, who was killed at the battle of the Opequan, and whose death General Sheridan felt extremely.

"These the tents
Which he frequents,"

and in such society he forgets his usual reticence, and talks by the hour about West Point life and "larks" on the Pacific Coast. Occasionally, when the old associations come back to the party very strongly, they lapse into the Indian tongue, which they all understand, and, with speech clothed in this disguise, they can safely revive recollections which, may be, if told in plain English, would astonish the audience, for it is only of late that they have been obliged to sustain the dignity of major-generals commanding.

Though always easy of approach, the general has little to say in busy times. Set teeth and a quick way tell when things do not go as they ought, and he has a manner on such occasions that stirs to activity all within sight, for a row seems brewing that nobody wants to be under when it bursts. Notwithstanding his handsome reputation for cursing, he is rather remarkably low-voiced, particularly on the field, where, as sometimes happens, almost everybody else is screaming. "Damn you, sir, don't yell at me," he once said to an officer who came galloping up with some bad news, and was roaring it out above the din of battle. In such moments the general leans forward on his horse's neck, and hunching his shoulders up to his ears, gives most softly spoken orders in a slow, deliberate way, as if there were niches for all the words in his hearer's memory, and they must be measured very carefully to fit exactly, that none of them be lost in the carrying. This is a pleasing way to have orders dealt out, especially under fire.

When he sees things going wrong in any part of the field, he has a trick of moving forward restlessly in his saddle, as if he would go and put them to rights if he could take leave of his better judgment and follow his inclination; but a serious check or reverse affects him peculiarly. To most temperaments disaster is disheartening, but it passes by General Sheridan as an eddy glides round a pier; his equanimity is not affected by it, and he is not depressed for a moment, for he is a man of much variety and quick resource, and to his aid comes a defiant spirit, which twinkles in his eye when he is called upon to retrieve disaster. Victor Hugo's brave Frenchman in the Old Guard at Waterloo had no more contempt for the enemy than he, but he shows it rather by a talent for ignoring defeat and compelling success than by permitting a useless sacrifice. He never would acknowledge to the most confidential recess of his own bosom that his command was past redemption, and there was nothing to do but go and die like a demigod. But it is not because he is impassive that he cannot be stampeded by reports or events, for he is keenly alive to the situation in whatever shape it presents itself. Show him an opening promising success, and he will go in and widen it while an impassive man would be thinking about it. But he is slow to confess defeat; a peculiar organization, so acute in most of its perceptions, and yet so dull in realizing failure. The prominence of this quality must be apparent to all who know anything of him in the war, where his wizard fingers snatched a great victory from the enemy just as they were passing it to history as theirs.

In aggressive and defensive warfare he is alike wary and cautious in regard to the protection of his lines and communications, and guards against surprise as if crediting his enemies with as much activity and invention as he himself possesses. Playing games all the time, no doubt, in his imagination with fancied foes in fancied places, he sees with unusual clearness any weakness in his own real positions, and prepares accordingly. And being almost as great a smoker as General Grant when actively employed in the field, and a constant cloud enveloping him in his busiest moments, it seems probable that smoke is an ally of military genius, and a medium through which the hostile array takes form and arranges itself for destruction; at any rate it is not known from what strange sources genius sometimes draws her inspirations, and something in this way may be claimed for cigars. Let us say so to justify the use of them, and hope that those who have not genius may perchance one day inhale some.

The general has a remarkable eye for topography, not only in using to the best advantage the peculiarities of the country through which he is campaigning, either for purposes of marching, assault, or defense, but he can foresee with accuracy, by studying a map, how far the country will be available for these purposes. His intelligent pursuit of Lee is due in a great measure to this accomplishment, for it enabled him to decide for himself, when lacking reliable information, as to what would be the most natural line of the enemy's retreat. The engineers have in him a rare customer for those wares which sometimes have tended to clog campaigns, for constant study of maps has often seemed to befog the student. They are responsible for many long marchings of weary troops, and for mistakes that have caused disaster when both could have been avoided, perhaps, by such simple inquiries as a solitary horseman would make, and troops go astray under the additional disadvantage that large bodies cannot rectify mistakes as a single horseman can; the ponderous length of a column *en route* is not to be twisted through by-ways and short-cuts, and cannot retrace its steps in every sort of road. To be good at topography, then, is to possess a most valuable quality as a campaigner, and General Sheridan has it in an uncommon degree, and prides himself on it somewhat, having come safely through with a few hap-hazard experiments in that line. When he was returning from his raid upon the Virginia Central Railroad, near Gordonsville, to rejoin General Grant, in June, 1864, he found at the White House some 700 wagons belonging to the cavalry, horse artillery, quartermaster's department, Sanitary Commission, Christian Commission, sutlers, and the other branches of the service, and it required considerable manœuvring to march this immense train of unwieldly transportation in such manner as should protect it from the rebellious cavalry of General Hampton, which was hanging upon our flank and hungrily regarding said wagons. We proposed to cross the Chickahominy at Providence Forge, and if a road to that point by way of New Kent Court House could be found, the trains could travel it securely, for our cavalry would cover the direct road to the Chickahominy and prevent the enemy from invading the little peninsula, in which New Kent Court House sits in judgment, between this river and the Pamunkey. The most diligent study of the maps failed to discover any indication of such a road, and no consecutive series of lines could be traced in that direction; equally diligent search failed to discover any one to the manor born who knew of any such outlet: but the interests of the service demanded that it should exist, and so, after mature deliberation and much pondering over maps, the commanding general decided that there *was* a road, *must* be a road. This conclusion being conclusive, the trains were started, and a staff officer was sent with General Getty (who happened to be returning to the army, convalescent from bad wounds received in the Wilderness, and had now command of the provisional brigade that escorted the wagons), and they two were charged with finding their way to the Chickahominy *via* New Kent Court House, by such avenues as could be discovered or manufactured. At that time the Court House was a deserted village; gaunt dogs were the only living beings for miles around, and they could give no geographical information; but perseverance was rewarded with success; a good wood-road was found, the trains reached the Chickahominy without delay, and the general's topographical bump was vindicated. This incident will illustrate, perhaps, the confident spirit of the man, as well as his intelligent comprehension of the features of a country.

He has been called ruthless and cruel because, in obedience to the orders of the officers appointed over him, he was compelled, by the stern necessities of war, to destroy property in the Shenandoah Valley, and to take from the war-ridden people there what their friends had left them of supplies for man and beast. As he rode down the Martinsburg Pike in his four-horse wagon, heels on the front seat, and smoking a cigar, while behind him his cavalry was destroying the provender that could not be carried away, the inhabitants of the valley doubtless regarded him as history regards the emperor who fiddled while Rome was burning, and would not now believe, what is the simple truth, that this destruction was distasteful to him, and that he was moved by the distress he was obliged to multiply upon these unfortunate people, whose evil fate had left them in the ruinous track of war so long. But the Shenandoah Valley was the well-worn pathway of invasion, and it became necessary that this long avenue leading to our homes should be stripped of the sustenance that rendered it possible to subsist an army there. This was apparent to all, but only resorted to when it had been satisfactorily demonstrated that so long as this pathway was strewed with flowers it would tempt to the Potomac such formidable bodies of the enemy as had periodically appeared upon its banks and demoralized the States of Maryland and Pennsylvania, to say nothing of the District of Columbia. It fell to General Sheridan to desolate this fertile valley, and the orders were carried out literally but not riotously, and so far as his authority could be exercised there was no unnecessary destruction. His kindliness has been abundantly exhibited to many in the enemy's country, on the march and about his encampments; but war is usually a bad business for property, and our war was not exceptional. Soldiers who are afraid to meet the dangers they would incur by assaulting the armed enemy in the field generally assault with violence everything that is defenseless, from henhouses to black women's earrings, and the peculiar mode of cavalry campaigning favored these evil-doers. Rations of all kinds run short very soon after cutting loose from a base of supplies, and foraging becomes necessary to the existence of the command; on long marches horses give out and fall by the roadside—Sheridan's milestones they came to be called,—and then the dismounted men, where the country will permit, follow the general direction of the column, and cut across lots when they find they save distance by leaving the road. They have also discovered that the best of the houses are away off out of sight, and with no officers to command and no humanity to control them, these generally worthless walkers perpetrate deeds for which the whole command gets credit, although the others would hang them with pleasure if they could. The good men will seldom lose their horses *en route*, for they nurse their failing footsteps by ingenious devices, while a bad soldier will sit upon his poor, tottering brute, until he pitch forward on to his head in the road, and never so much as cast overboard a frying-pan or a stolen ham to lighten ship and get his craft into port. Then he goes off and plunders. "Pity 'tis 'tis true," but, as a soldier said, you cannot expect all the virtues for thirteen dollars a month.

By-and-by the infantry comes along, and the stragglers of that arm beat up the country-side for pelf, and finding none, join in the wail of the natives, and in cursing "Sheridan's Robbers." The cavalry men accepted this soubriquet, and the best of them rather delighted in it. When they were passing through the streets of Washington just before the grand review, somebody on the pavement asked, "What command is that?" and a dozen voices from the ranks replied, "Sheridan's Robbers!" and thus the commander's name was familiarly linked with a scandalous title, which, however well deserved by a worthless minority of the troops, owed nothing to the precept or example of the general himself, who had firmly set his face against plundering and marauding, as his numerous orders on that subject and the persons of captured depredators will bear testimony. He appreciated at its proper value the vital importance of maintaining strict discipline in every condition of warfare, to preserve his command from that demoralization in battle which goes hand in hand with the spirit of lawlessness, and nobody ever saw him unnecessarily harass the hostile people among whom he was campaigning, even when he knew that every house was the home of a bushwhacker, and that in every wood-road guerrillas lay in wait for life. In fact, our armies were always wonderfully tolerant of those cruel enemies, though many tired soldiers, who had fallen behind the column on a long day's march, and many staff officers on duty within our lines, had become their victims. General Sheridan had three of his own staff killed by guerrillas in the Shenandoah Valley, shot without warning or a chance for their lives: Colonel Tolles, the able chief quartermaster, young Meigs of the engineers, who was making a brilliant reputation in his department, and Dr. Oehlschlager, the efficient medical inspector of the Army of the Shenandoah, these all fell because in our passive way we had submitted to be murdered rather than destroy, and had not made bushwacking "odious" and the retribution terrible. Almost everywhere in Virginia the staff officers felt that they carried their lives in their hands together with their dispatches, and if a twig cracked by the roadside it seemed ominous of bullets and sudden death. But no special steps were ever taken to eradicate this crying evil, while the provost marshals hardly could supply the demand for guards to protect the houses and property of those who indulged in these practices undisturbed. That such a state of affairs should exist about him and the people be still permitted to remain at home, proves that General Sheridan has "charity for all," and that it does not gratify him to desolate and lay waste.

A little bit more of personal description, and then we will move out against the enemy. In the field, even in the hottest weather, the general wears in part the uniform of his grade in its most exacting and uncomfortable form, to wit, a double-breasted frock-coat; pantaloons outside his boots, strapped down, and chafing against small brass spurs, one of which, broken short off at the heel, did duty for several months to the satisfaction of the general, and doubtless to the satisfaction of the horses. He avoids the army hat for officers, which is not becoming to every style of beauty, and the cap, which seems to be in the interests of the elements, affording no protection against the sun's rays, the visor bending upward, forming a water-course for the conveyance of rain-drops to the inside of the wearer's shirt-collar. These facts beget variety in head costume, and General Sheridan usually appears in the soft civilian's pork-pie of the period, which for various uses, from an umbrella to a nightcap, has no equal. However, it is not the intention of this narration to advertise hats, and the reader has been patiently expecting something about the last campaign. So now "to horse!"

CHAPTER II.

FROM THE SHENANDOAH TO THE JAMES.

THE last campaign against Lee may be said to have been inaugurated when General Sheridan started with his cavalry from Winchester, Virginia, on the 27th of February, 1865, with a sort of *carte blanche* of destruction as to the enemy's supply depots and communications. The general's instructions looked to his crossing the James River above Richmond, and his possible junction with the command of General Sherman somewhere in North Carolina; but the swollen condition of the James and the destruction of the bridges prevented his crossing, and thus were thrown in his way opportunities for distinction which could scarcely have been waiting for him on the other side of Lee's army. It is not worth while though to speculate as to whether the last campaign of the Army of the Potomac would have proved so sharp, short, and decisive without the cavalry in advance and General Sheridan for a pioneer, and so it is useless to imagine in what way he and his cavalry could have won glory with Sherman. The events as we find them are so satisfactory that it is needless to resort to the solace of dissatisfaction—speculations as to what might have been.

General Sheridan's command on this expedition consisted of the first cavalry division, under Brevet Major-General Wesley Merritt, and the third cavalry division, under Brevet Major-General Geo. A. Custer, to whose division was added one brigade of the cavalry of the old army of West Virginia, under Colonel Capehart. The story of their successful raid is not important here, except to follow their trail and see where they join the Army of the Potomac. They left Winchester on a damp, disagreeable morning, all the roads but the turnpike being almost impassable; the huge blocks with which patrician wisdom had paved the old Virginia town were glib as glass, and one of the staff got a very bad fall with his horse, his own leg being broken and badly crushed against the enormous paving stones in front of the headquarters. This drizzly promise of the morning was fulfilled, and rain fell heavily with the evening, drenching the command, swelling the streams, deepening the roads, etc., according to the manner of rains in Virginia. But the spirits of the bold dragoons were not dampened, and they felt lively enough to push on to Waynesborough to the camp of General Jubal Early, late of the Confederacy, upon whom the brilliant Custer fell with his division, and soon had his guns, and men, and *matériel*, and would have had him but that he had sufficient presence of mind to absent his person when he found how things were going. This was General Early's last appearance in public life, and it seems that he did not cease to fly until he had crossed the ocean on wings of panic, and now takes heart of distance and tries to prove that he fought the campaign of the Shenandoah Valley, from first to last, with a few thousand less men than got into the hands of our provost marshal during some slight casualties that befell General Early in those days.

Early's command at Waynesborough being now dispersed or captured, and the prisoners having been sent off to Winchester in charge of a trusty officer (Colonel Thompson of the First New Hampshire Cavalry) and a guard of some five hundred men, General Sheridan proceeded to occupy Charlottesville. The mayor brought out the keys and politely offered him the freedom of the city, which was accepted, and then a halt was called to await the transportation, for the rains had continued and the floods had come, but the wagons had not. Then on again toward Lynchburg and the James River; rapid detours being made in every direction by small parties striking at supplies and communications, and returning to the main column again in a boomerang sort of a way that was as confusing to the inhabitants and to the enemy as it was destructive of property. When it was found impossible to cross the James River, attention was for a while directed to the demolition of the James River and Kanawha Canal, which Washington is said to have projected for the benefit of his native State. Here State interest had to give way for the common cause of the Union, and a modern patriot had to undo the work which the patriot of the olden time had proposed, because the State which the latter would have benefited had failed to follow some other good advice of his, more important to its prosperity than the James River Canal. In a patriotic way, then, this line of supply was completely interrupted, and its bed was so upturned that it hardly yet can lie there as of old. The River James, swollen with the high tide of rebellion and hurrying proudly down to its capital, was turned aside in mid-career and made an unwilling agent in destroying its innocent offspring, and then escaping as quickly as possible from this compulsory infanticide it dashed over the canal's red banks again, bearing on its bosom the stains which told the inhabitants of Richmond of the dark deeds enacting about them, and giving them warning of coming events.

When the ingenious destruction corps could devise no further damage here, the command turned off to try its hand upon a railroad or two. All the time the rains had descended—the floodgates of the clouds were up and the water kept pouring through; the roads became dreadful, horses sank almost to their bellies, and wagon-wheels revolved upon the hubs. Although nothing short of a flotilla seemed likely to ride out the storm, the cavalry rode on hopefully, and came safely to harbor at the White House, on the Pamunkey, where supplies were furnished them, and where the March winds blew them dry again. But so much mud had been bad for the horses, and more than three thousand had fallen by the roadside, or, barely reaching camp, had to be turned over to the fostering care of the quartermaster's department, on account of that dreadful scalding which swells their legs as the elephantiasis sometimes does the limbs of human beings.

Immediately upon his arrival at this depot, General Sheridan reported to General Grant, at City Point, for orders. The lieutenant-general must have been pleased to receive this dispatch from his enterprising coadjutor, for had General Sheridan turned back from the impassable James and retraced his steps to Winchester, he could not have been blamed, and indeed it would probably have occurred to nobody to blame him, as nothing was then foreseen of what was to happen a little later. His meandering march, terminating at the White House, was the child of his own fertile imagination, not the offspring perhaps of a very clear idea in regard to what precisely would result from this "friendly move," but certainly the birth of a keen appreciation of the military status and a praiseworthy desire to place his command where it would be most available for the purposes for which he commanded it. By choosing this course he voluntarily forsook his large department of the Middle Military Division, and put himself in the field at the head of two cavalry divisions, headquarters in the saddle, and, applying for a new situation, made no stipulations for himself, and no objection to going into the country. It was quite patriotic, to say the least of it, this eagerness to crush the unholy rebellion.

When the cavalry had rested and refitted, and was ready to move, General Sheridan, leaving General Merritt to conduct the column from the White House to the James River, rode across the Peninsula and visited General Grant at City Point, where also he found President Lincoln, who had gone to be near the army in the last great effort for which all were preparing, and for an opportunity of "communing with his captains of the war." The President was established on the beautiful little steamer "Mary Martin," which had been tender (and no wonder) to a delightful party under charge of General Meade, whose pleasant visit had been cut short by a rude attack upon our lines. On the morning that the cavalry reached the James, Mr. Lincoln sailed up the river, in company with General Sheridan and the lieutenant-general, to see our command cross at the bridge below the Dutch Gap Canal. Looking from the window of the steamer's cabin, the President appeared like a man whose heart was sick with hope deferred, and full of anxiety for the coming campaign. Everybody felt afraid that Lee would steal away, for every hour must have been full of apprehension for his line of retreat, while every moment he must have dreaded an overwhelming attack upon his front. Behind him Sherman, whom nothing could stop, was closing in; in front, Sheridan had been able to roam over Virginia and join the armies on the James, and nothing could be spared to hinder him; but, hoping against hope, like sleepy flies Lee's army saw the encircling web, and still stayed on to be entrapped. Seeing the troubles besetting Lee, all were alarmed lest he should pocket his pride, abandon the capital, postpone his evil day, and perhaps achieve some temporary advantage by rapidly joining Johnston in North Carolina, with whom his communications were still intact.

It was the hope of the army, as well as of the President, that Lee's evil day should not be thus postponed, but that then and there, in Virginia, where the struggle had begun and been most fiercely maintained, it should be terminated, so far as the Army of the Potomac and her allies on the James were concerned. The troops demanded this in the name of poetical justice, and all patriots desired it with intense craving. So long as Lee could be kept at Petersburg by stratagem or force, or by his own fool-hardiness, so long the people and the army could hope for a decisive and brilliant campaign, and hope would keep alive the enthusiasm which the chances of success inspired; but if he should decamp, enthusiasm would give place to lassitude; again the desponding would see lions in the path; Lee would find hosts of believers in the bragging assertion that if Richmond were captured he could wage war in the mountains for twenty years; and it would seem so much like the old, old story, that the stoutest would despair in contemplating the campaign that would ensue,—transports required to ship troops here, railroads to be repaired to supply them there, long marches, long halts, bad climate, bad roads, hard fighting, and hard luck; then more men and more money. On the other hand, there really seemed a prospect that Lee would be "bagged" for positively the last time, if he should remain until we could get ready to move against him. Victory was almost within our grasp, and "victory's daughter"— Peace.

> "Longing for her, our spirits wilt
> Like shipwrecked men's, on rafts, for water."

And so we almost trembled as the rumbling of the hoofs and the clanging of the sabers on the bridge were echoed by the up-river hills, for we feared that the reverberation might reach the ears of Lee and wake him from his trance, and start him up crying for his horse. He slept well through it all though, and we camped that night on the windy south bank of the James.

Next morning, March 27th, we were off bright and early for the left flank of the Army of the Potomac, where we found our old friends of Gregg's cavalry division from whom we had parted when ordered to the Shenandoah Valley with the other two divisions of the corps; but we missed the golden beard of the imperturbable General Gregg, who had so admirably commanded this superb division, and who, for some pressing private reasons, had now resigned from the army. On the day of our arrival, General Crook assumed command of the division, and reported to General Sheridan, thus reuniting the old cavalry corps under its most famous commander.

CHAPTER III.

SHERIDAN'S CAVALRY.

BEFORE starting again upon the war-path, it may not be amiss to say a few words in regard to the cavalry as it stood at this time in the estimation of the army and of the country, and of the steps by which it was brought into favor, if only as a poor tribute to the memory of a gallant few, who, ardently seeking to distinguish their arm of the service, lost their lives before it had gained its best repute.

It was quite the thing early in the war to sneer at mounted troops. A distinguished major-general is said to have asked, after an engagement, if anybody had seen a dead cavalryman; and very likely nobody had, for in those primitive days the major-generals themselves had not the least idea of how to go to work to get cavalry killed, and when any did fall they fell through a laudable desire to do something for the country and for their own reputation, and not because they had been ordered to do anything hazardous. For a long while they had no united organization; on the Peninsula, under McClellan, nobody in particular commanded the cavalry: General Stoneman had some, General P. St. George

Cook had considerable, General Averell had a little, and the corps commanders had each a supply; and thus it happened that we were all confused and helpless when General Stuart made his raid with the muscular Prussian who writes for *Blackwood's Magazine,* and a few other troops taken for the purpose of admiring the Prussian's prowess; we presented the lamentable spectacle in *our* command of grazing our horses in the finest clover, in an open country, in broad daylight, while Stuart rode by within a mile or two, the Prussian brandishing his thirsty blade, to which, by all accounts, Excalibur was a poor affair. After they had put many miles between us, one brigade went tumbling after them as far as Tunstall's Station, and thence one regiment was sent in pursuit, with orders to inflict such damage upon the enemy, when overtaken, as should warn him against attempting a second time to circumvent the Army of the Potomac. If this lone regiment had overtaken the raiders, it is horrible to dwell upon the certain results; and it is some compensation for our disgraceful performances as a body, that, as individuals, we escaped from the Prussian, for he would have broken us in pieces as his ancestors the Kaisers broke horseshoes with their fists, as witness the shattered fragments in the Green Vaults at Dresden; but we escaped that fate, and went slowly back to camp, and still struggled on in the unequal conflict.

In the great engagements of the seven days the cavalry did nothing of signal service. One regiment charged gallantly at the battle of Gaines's Mills, only to be scattered and broken against the solid lines of the enemy's infantry, who no more regarded this feeble onset than the rocks give way before the washing of the surf; General Stoneman, with a portion of the cavalry, was cut off from the main body of the army, and was ordered by Fitz John Porter, from Gaines's Mills, to make his way to Yorktown, and thence rejoin the army as circumstances should permit. And this movement incidentally was of service in leading astray the enemy under Jackson, whose infantry followed Stoneman's column as far as the hills overlooking the White House, whence they retraced their steps to pursue McClellan across the Chickahominy; but the credit to the cavalry would have been greater if this result had been designed.

In the Maryland campaign General Pleasonton had a couple of good brigades, and was energetic and successful in pushing after the enemy toward the Antietam; but during the great battle nothing aggressive was attempted by his cavalry, unless it was the gallop across the bridge on the Sharpsburg Pike, under a galling artillery fire, and driving away the enemy's guns. After that was done, the troopers went into position along the creek, and sat upon their horses, under shelter of some rising ground, until the sun went down, all kinds of missiles humming over them all day almost harmlessly.

After the battle, the scattering process was again resorted to, and Stuart was again tempted to try a raid round our army. It is true that he accomplished very little besides the ruin of his own horses. He was like the wind on a frolic, which did great damage to "old women's bonnets and ginger-bread stalls," but he did not much affect the prospects of the war, and did not drive the Northern army from the field. The ignominy, however, was none the less on this account when we discovered that no cavalry could be concentrated to intercept him.

On the whole, though, the mounted troops must have raised themselves a peg in this campaign, for we find General McClellan unable to move across the Potomac for want of them; and it is a fact that they were in a very bad way just then, by reason of a terrible disease of the hoof, which affected the horses—a disease brought about by bad feed, turnpike dust, overheating, and many other causes, perhaps guessed at by everybody; but the malady was remedied by none until it had run its course.

After crossing the Potomac, the cavalry, under Generals Pleasonton and Averell, took the advance very creditably, always encountering the enemy's cavalry successfully, and never calling upon our infantry for support.

At Fredericksburg there was no use for horsemen, and very few crossed the Rappahannock during the engagement. General Bayard made a reconnoissance with his brigade on the plains where Franklin was, on the left, but he could do no good where the enemy could see his every movement and he could see no enemy; and, after this gallant young general was killed, the brigade was withdrawn to the north bank of the river.

After Fredericksburg, General Hooker lifted the cavalry over the stile by consolidating it. A cavalry corps was formed, and General Stoneman was assigned to the command; and then for the first time it was realized what a capital mounted force there was. Superb regiments seemed to creep out of every defile within the lines of the army. Three divisions were organized under Generals Pleasonton, Averell, and Gregg, and General Buford commanded the brigade of regulars. When President Lincoln came down to the army for a grand review, nobody was more astonished than the troops themselves when they saw the face of the country swarm with cavalry, and apparently an endless stream of horsemen pouring from every avenue leading to the parade-ground. The enemy, regarding the magnificent mass from the heights of St. Marie across the river, must have felt a slight reaction from the victorious glow of Fredericksburg, seeing that the Yankees were not all dead yet.

Averell's division made a very handsome dash across Kelly's Ford on St. Patrick's day, and then came Stoneman's raid, and Chancellorsville. Success at the great battle was necessary to Stoneman's success; failure at the battle rendered Stoneman's best efforts futile; for he was dispatched to the rear of Lee to annoy him as he retreated, to destroy his communications, to block up the roads, to get between the beaten enemy and his capital, and, in the words of the orders given General Stoneman, to "fight, fight, fight." Cutting loose from the army, he followed his instructions as well as he could; but the other programme as laid down was not entirely executed, owing to unforeseen circumstances, and in a week or more General Stoneman found himself many miles from his friends, and could get no tidings of the defeated enemy. Then he had to get back the best way he could, in the most drenching weather, and over the most frightful roads. On his safe return, patriotic efforts were made to cheer up the desponding people with glowing stories of his achievements; the illustrated papers had him depicted on a fiery charger, with his scabbard on the wrong side, pointing with his sword at miles of railroad bridges wrapped in flame, and correspondents exhausted imagination in describing the ruin he had scattered broadcast. Shrewd Mr. Lincoln, however, saw that the raid was not a crushing blow to the rebellion, and he had his little joke over it, sadly enough no doubt, though it is probable that he did not fully comprehend how fatal to the success of Stoneman had been the failure at Chancellorsville. In that battle General Pleasonton did excellent execution with his command. At a critical moment, when Jackson had stampeded the Eleventh Corps and was carrying everything before him, Pleasonton's cavalry stood fast, and, catching up some flying artillery, opposed a front before which Jackson halted and afterward met his death.

After Chancellorsville, there was a good deal of bad blood in military quarters; great promise had been followed by but small fulfillment, and scape-goats were needed on whom to fasten blunders. Generals Stoneman and Averell figured in that capacity, and General Pleasonton succeeded to the command of the corps. At this time it was known that Stuart was getting ready his cavalry for a great raid into Pennsylvania, and his camp near Brandy Station was busy with preparation; so General Pleasonton, on the 9th of June, 1863, went across the Rappahannock to look for a fight in which to cripple the enemy's horse and send them into hospital for repairs. This was successfully accomplished; from daylight to sunset the championship was hotly contested by the rival troopers, and our men won the belt, and held it against all comers from that time. The seeker for disabled cavalrymen could have found one thousand one hundred killed and wounded of ours on that stricken plain,—

"And the steed with broken rein ran free."

Stuart staggered under the shock, and thereby failed in his whole campaign; for he was so late in starting that we got across his path at Aldie, when he was bound for the Potomac at Edward's Ferry, ten days later, and General Pleasonton pressed him back to Middletown, and drove him through Upperville to Ashby's Gap—a glorious series of engagements for our cavalry—and we bottled him up in the valley until we had no object in keeping him there longer. When he got out he was much too late to do any harm, as we had got over the Potomac first; and General Lee's report of the Gettysburg campaign proves how useless to him was his mounted force.

At Frederick City a new division joined the corps, and was put under General Kilpatrick, with Farnsworth and Custer for brigade commanders. This division ran foul of Stuart in Hanovertown, Pennsylvania, and had a handsome little fight, while General Buford with his command, in advance of General Reynolds's corps, opened the ball at Gettysburg, and is entitled to the highest praise for his very distinguished services on that occasion. During the great battle of the two succeeding days the cavalry on both flanks fought hard, Gregg on the right repulsing Stuart's fierce assault, made with the hope of reaching our rear, and Kilpatrick and Merritt on the left charging the enemy's infantry, and keeping a large force busy there. After the battle, there were raids on wagon trains and dashes at the rebel rear-guard.

The cavalry was now an acknowledged element, and there never was any trouble in finding enough for it to do; and the mounted men were beginning to earn their rations, and enjoy a night's rest when they could get it. They could hold up their heads among their fellow-soldiers of the other arms of the service, for they now swept the roads clear for the infantry march and only drew off to the flanks when general engagements were to the fore, and then kept their three-inch rifled guns and their carbines rattling away against the ribs of the enemy's lines, getting their own saddles emptied, and filling the fields with dead and wounded enough to satisfy anybody.

It is not necessary to follow them through the brilliant encounters of this fall in Culpepper County, in the retreat to Centreville, and back again to the Rapidan and Mine Run, or through the hard picketing of the cold, wet winter, when they did an amount of work that nobody can appreciate by a home fireside.

In the spring General Pleasonton was relieved of command, together with other generals of the Army of the Potomac who were supposed not to pull kindly with General Meade, and General Sheridan assumed command of the cavalry corps. Kilpatrick, who had made a hard and unsuccessful raid during the winter, went to the West at this time, and was succeeded by General Wilson. The brave and brilliant General Buford had died in the fall, and, among many others, those gallant officers Colonel B. F. (Grimes) Davis and General Farnsworth had given up their lives in hand-to-hand encounters at the head of their brigades. General Torbert now commanded the first division, and General Gregg still retained the second. General Sheridan immediately brought the cavalry into still greater favor by his engagements in the Wilderness and fighting raid to the James River, in which General Stuart was killed, at Yellow Tavern. Some of the best-contested cavalry battles of the war followed his return, Gregg at Hawes's Shop, and Torbert at Cold Harbor, winning the admiration of the army.

Then came the long ride to Trevilian Station and back, and the sharp fighting there.

Wilson's raid toward Danville was a failure in some respects, but General Grant says the damage inflicted upon the enemy's railroads compensated for his own losses.

At Deep Bottom, on the James, we achieved a great success, fighting infantry as at Cold Harbor; and all this time most of the engagements had been fought dismounted. "Prepare to fight on foot!" was the usual order after a little skirmishing had developed the enemy, and the horses hardly knew anything of the battles, while their riders were following the flag through swamps and brakes and virgin forest,—not legitimate work for mounted troops, perhaps, but a good nursery for soldiers; it inured them to hardships, and taught them that their duty was to fight the enemy wherever found; that if the rebellion was not to be ridden down, it must be trampled under foot; and the cavalry, with patience, gallantry, and devotion, followed this teaching, and rendered themselves capable of profiting by the glorious opportunities which later campaigns afforded.

We now found that Gregg's excellent division — although envying the good fortune of their old comrades who had been plucking laurels on horseback in the battles of the Shenandoah Valley—had increased the reputation of the cavalry in some desperate engagements, dismounted, in the woods at Deep Bottom and on the Boydton Plank Road; and so, when the old corps was reunited, its blended honors were not surpassed in any corps of the army.

Now the troopers were spoken of always with respect, often with admiration. They had shown themselves the peers of the best of the infantry side by side with them on hard-fought fields, and artillery asked no better support. They had been tried in every phase of warfare, and never been found wanting. Their depleted ranks had been filled with the best of volunteers—drafted men and substitutes being seldom put into cavalry—and the new men quickly fell into the old men's ways and boldly followed their file-leaders into battle. The whole corps was animated by the best spirit, anxious for victory and willing to go through anything to secure it; self-reliant, and believing in their commanders, they expected success, and would not be denied wherever it was possible.

CHAPTER IV.

FEELING LEE'S RIGHT FLANK.

At the head of this magnificent command, possessing the entire confidence of every man who followed, General Sheridan rode out from his camp on the morning of the 29th of March, 1865, bound for Dinwiddie Court House, on the Boydton Plank Road, and bound to crush the rebellion, so far as one man by precept and example could effect that desired consummation. He was under the immediate orders of Lieutenant-General Grant, and commanded the cavalry as a separate army, as General Meade commanded the Army of the Potomac and General Ord the Army of the James. His subordinate commanders were General Merritt, commanding the first and third cavalry divisions from the Shenandoah Valley—General Devin commanding the former, and General Custer the latter—and General Crook, commanding the second division (Gregg's old). In the first division the brigades were commanded by General Gibbs, Colonel Stagg, and Colonel Fitzhugh; in the second division, by Generals Davies, Irvine Gregg, and Smith; and in the third division, by Colonels Pennington, Wells, and Capehart.

General Sheridan had been ordered to get out toward Dinwiddie Court House, and the enemy's left and rear, as best he could. General Grant wrote: "move your cavalry at as early an hour as you can, and without being confined to any particular road or roads." The avowed object of the movement of the armies was to get the enemy out of his intrenched works, where he could be attacked with some chance of success. If the enemy should come out, General Sheridan was to "go in," and was assured that he would be properly supported; if the enemy should not come out, the general was to go on a raid, and cry havoc along the enemy's Southside and Danville Railroads. It was a Micawber-like move at first, partly to help along the cavalry, partly in expectation that something would turn up. The Confederacy was upturned shortly, but just on this particular morning nobody had a very clear idea of what was going to happen, and General Grant himself apparently did not come to a realizing sense of the possibilities within reach, and did not feel grasping, until he got well out into the country that night, when he was seized with a desire of "ending the matter."

Meanwhile, General Sheridan, keeping to himself his reflections and hopes, whatever they might be, was carrying out his original orders in a literal manner; and getting up *very* early in the morning (as early as he can being a good deal earlier than anybody else wants to), had crossed the Jerusalem Plank Road, and was exercising his topographical genius in finding roads in general and not particular, leading in the direction in which his face was set.

Whoever has traveled the highways of Dinwiddie County, Virginia, in the melting days of spring, has probably recollections of black soil appearing here and there, islands in ponds of black water fringed with green; whoever has left the highways for a short-cut will remember how his horse broke through the upper crust and found apparently nothing below but space. We all drew sanguine auguries from this, and wished that the soil might be emblematical of the cause, since in Virginia the soil and the cause were almost synonymous; and so we labored on hopefully, every man for himself and his horse, across the Weldon Railroad at Reims's Station, where twisted rails and strong lines of earthworks told of the old moves and the old hard fights. But somehow this place is unpleasant, for it reminds us all of how our present expedition may be nothing more than the old story of flanks extended, attacked, defended, and intrenched; something gained of course, a pawn moved up into a good place, shutting up a little of the scope the adversary had, but not a checkmate, which we are after *this* time, and are therefore rather easier in our minds when we have passed out beyond the old lines, sent out our advance-guard, and got into the undiscovered country.

At Rowanty Creek, or Run, as Virginians commonly call their little streams, we found the bridge down, and it was necessary to rebuild it. Experience teaches, and our command had had much experience in bridge-building. The First Maine Cavalry, lumbermen and rail-splitters, could knock up a bridge over an ordinary stream while the horses were being watered, and plenty of other regiments could swing an awful axe, and we soon had this bridge up and were crossing the Rowanty by fours. The field-report of effective strength was verified here by actual count, and the command was found to number— General Merritt's command 5700; Crook's 3300: total—9000 effective men and horses.

On the other side of the Rowanty our advance caught sight of a small picket-force of the enemy's cavalry, and, giving chase rapidly, captured a few of them; and meanwhile our scouts were out after information in all directions, and we were constantly getting news of the enemy's movements.

These scouts were a fine body of some sixty men selected from the whole cavalry corps, and commanded by Major H. H. Young, of the Second Rhode Island Infantry, an excellent officer, fond of adventure, brave, and a good disciplinarian; he had attracted the attention of General

Sheridan by his gallantry in the Shenandoah Valley, and was assigned to duty on his staff, and ordered to organize his present command. As a general thing, scouts are perfectly worthless. They are usually plausible fellows who go out to the picket-line and lie on the ground all night under a tree, and come back to headquarters in the morning and lie there, giving wonderful reports about the enemy, fearing no contradiction. They swagger frightfully when small towns are occupied and there are any natives to astonish; then they turn out in the full uniform of the enemy, being surrounded by friends, and, with two pistols in the belt and one in each boot, these walking arsenals walk into everything that does not belong to them and help themselves. Young's men were differently managed, and were of great service. They were much more afraid of the general and of the major than they were of the enemy, for the general has a way of cross-examining that is fatal to a lie, and as Young was constantly off in the enemy's country himself, his men never knew but that he had been following their trail, so there was no use trying to shut up his eye, as a scout would say. These men had been with the major on several successful expeditions and in some desperate fights. They had taken Harry Gilmor out of his bed and confiscated the pistols on his pillow, without disturbing his command; in the Shenandoah Valley they had swept the picket-line of the enemy and cut their way through the reserves, losing several killed and wounded in the attempt. They knew the major and each other, and Young knew them, and they had that mutual confidence which is vital to a party of this sort. They were like what romance tells us of Marion's men; but after the experience of the late war an impression steals over the mind that Marion's men were *really* bushwackers—hard names to call revolutionary heroes, but their Southern compatriots throw suspicion upon them by an aptitude that must have been "bred in the bone." Young's men dressed in the Confederate uniform habitually; mingled with the people, told them the news and got the news of them in return; cursed the Yankees, and drank stirrup-cups of apple-jack to their discomfiture; warned the host against their coming, and then rode away, while one of their number quickly slipped back through unfrequented paths and communicated the latest from the front to the general commanding. At night, while the troops rested, Young and his men would be miles away in every direction, and during the day we would pick them up at every cross-road with the best intelligence from right and left. The men were well paid for this hazardous work, and often received a bonus for special acts of daring and good service; and the major was compensated by his chances of distinction and the general's good opinion. He came to be well known in the sections where we campaigned, and those people who would acknowledge to a curiosity to see anything in the shape of a Yankee would ask to have Young pointed out.

At the Rowanty we learned from the prisoners and the scouts that a considerable body of the enemy's cavalry was marching on roads parallel with us on the other side of Stony Creek, pushing apparently for Dinwiddie Court House, to intercept us; so we moved on rapidly and gained that point, and the rebellious column let us alone when the uncaptured portion of their pickets galloped away from the court-house, and, dashing across the Stony Creek by the Boydton Plank Road bridge, informed their friends on the other side that Sheridan's cavalry was there. A party of our men quickly secured the bridge, tore up the planks, and made other arrangements for disputing the passage; but no attempt to cross was made by the enemy, who accepted the situation and hurried on to secure their connection with their own army, and to get between us and the Southside Railroad. Meanwhile we peacefully occupied Dinwiddie Court House, and went into camp in that vicinity.

In Virginia court-houses mean towns, and the towns are principally court-houses; here, however, there was a hotel thrown in, and a couple of cottages by way of outskirts. Perhaps there were three; there is no intention to be unjust to

Dinwiddie, and it is more than a year since we were there. Yes, there were three. There was the long, low mansion with a leaky piazza, in the hollow on the right; the little house on the hill, where we all took breakfast, for which the man took a dollar a head; and the brick-house by the temple of justice, which looked like a school-house, but probably was not. We established ourselves at the Dinwiddie Hotel,—hotel no longer except in name and in legend, for nobody ever passed by now but straggling cavalrymen, and cooking for them was reported to be not remunerative. Some of the pickets had slept there, though, for all the beds in the unoccupied rooms of the house were topsy-turvy,—and such beds! the feelings of the Northern matron would have been too great for utterance in contemplating them, and as for sleeping in them—even we were not reduced to that extremity: so we wrapped ourselves up in our martial cloaks and lay down, supperless, upon the floor, with chairs for pillows; supperless, because far away toward the Weldon Railroad our wagons were toiling painfully through the mud, getting out of one hole only to find another, while the quartermasters and Custer's division manfully endeavored to bring them on by putting the shoulder to the wheel, by calling on Jupiter, and by corduroying.

During the evening, to help matters along and give affairs a cheerful aspect, it began to rain: first a Scotch mist, then unsteady showers, and then a pour, as if the equinox, hurrying through the elements, had kicked over the water-buckets.

About this time General Grant was seized with the desire " to end the matter before going back." His illogical mind failed to be affected by the logic of events, failed to perceive that things were looking about as badly as they could for accomplishing anything, and so he sent a dispatch to General Sheridan countermanding his conditional orders in regard to the raid upon the Southside and Danville Railroads, and directing him to find the enemy's right and rear as soon as possible. Wishing to have a perfectly clear idea of General Grant's proposed plan of ending the matter, General Sheridan, soon after daylight on the 30th, mounted his gray pacer (captured from Breckenridge's adjutant-general at Missionary Ridge), and paced rapidly over to the headquarters of the lieutenant-general, taking two or three staff officers, with a dozen men for an escort. This little party raised an immense commotion on the picket-line of the army, and only after such persevering dumb-show as the friendly Friday made to Robinson Crusoe was it permitted to approach. Once inside, the pacer was let out again, and rein was drawn only when the horses slumped to their bellies in the quicksand-field where General Grant had pitched his tent, from which he regarded the tempest with derision.

About this time things certainly looked rather

blue to a superficial observer; the troops, just out of comfortable winter quarters, cowered under their scant shelters, or dragged themselves slowly along to their place in line, clogged with mud and weighed down with the drenching rain. In every by-way and in every field wagons were hopelessly imbedded in the glutinous soil. Drivers and mules had given it up, and the former smoked their pipes calmly under the wagons, while the latter turned tail to the storm and clustered around the feed-box, where they had put their heads together from habit, for there was nothing in the box to eat, and they *must* have been asses if they hoped the forage-wagons would get to the front that day. General Sheridan, water dripping from every angle of his face and clothes, was ushered into the presence and councils of the lieutenant-general, and between them they soon settled that, as it was within the limits of horse possibility for cavalry to move, they would move a little and see what came of it, if only to pass the time, for on a day like this the most ardent man must find employment or he will begin to think that he is a helpless party to a fiasco, which it must be acknowledged we all appeared to be just then. The only thing probably that could have amused the company on that inauspicious morning would have been an excited horseman straining through the treacherous soil, waving his hat, and crying out that Lee would surrender to Grant one hundred miles from there in ten days from date. That would have been extremely amusing, and the toughest veteran would have smiled grimly.

Very hopeful, but somewhat incredulous, were the veterans, and it was rather their fashion to scoff in the last year of the war. There were precedents for all sorts of campaigns except "the last," and the old troops were somewhat skeptical when that was predicted. They had something of the feeling of the man in "Used Up," who has been everywhere and seen everything—been up Mount Vesuvius, looked down the crater and found nothing in it. Lee had escaped them by only so much as Tam O'Shanter's mare escaped at the bridge, and possibly for the reason that armies like witches are balked by streams, as the Potomac and Rappahannock would seem to testify. They had been in Burnside's "mud movement," and looking on this picture and on that they discovered the counterfeit presentment of two brothers, so far as it was given to them to see; but the lieutenant-general and General Sheridan had not been in the other mud movement, and they are not men of routine to care for precedent, so the latter got into his wet saddle again, said good morning to the lieutenant-general as chirpily as if the elements were smiling, and sent off a staff officer by a short-cut to find General Merritt, on the road from Dinwiddie to Five Forks, and tell him to move out a little farther and stir up the animals.

The enemy's cavalry, which had been marching parallel with us the day before, had kept along the right bank of Stony Creek until they had passed beyond the Boydton Plank Road, and then had crossed over to the White Oak Road by the nearest route, in order to place themselves between us and the Southside Railroad, to which there is a direct road leading from Dinwiddie Court House through Five Forks and across Hatcher's Run. The White Oak Road was the prolongation of the right flank of the enemy's line protecting Petersburg, and was important to be guarded by them on that account also.

On this morning, as stated, General Merritt was posted on the Five Forks Road, and was about midway between that point and Dinwiddie Court House; General Gibbes, with the reserve brigade, had the advance, and was immediately moved out in obedience to General Sheridan's order. The leading regiments, Sixth Pennsylvania and Second Massachusetts Cavalry, had hardly passed through their picket-line when they became engaged with the enemy's cavalry, and a sharp skirmish ensued, in which Colonel Leiper, Sixth Pennsylvania Cavalry, commanding these two regiments, drove the enemy handsomely nearly to Five Forks, carrying a line of temporary breastworks, and developed a heavy force too strong for his command.

This reconnoissance was deemed satisfactory, as demonstrating the intention of the enemy to hold the White Oak Road, and a general engagement being impracticable and useless, owing to the condition of the weather and roads rendering co-operation by the infantry impossible, General Gibbes's brigade was slowly withdrawn to its original position, and the enemy, satisfied to be let alone, remained quiet for the rest of the day.

At dark we all sought the shelter of the Dinwiddie Hotel again, and the wagons still being reported far off in the slough, betook our hungry selves to music to while away the dreary hours. For the hotel had a piano, a relic of better days, rather unstrung, and a little off in tone perhaps, but good enough to sound chords for a chorus, for voices are full when some other things are empty. Lovely ladies assisted too—ladies who had fled from Charleston to Petersburg, and from Petersburg to Dinwiddie, to keep out of harm's way, and who now particularly requested us not to fight a battle near the Coat House, as they called it. Their gentlemen who had been on picket there had promised them not to fight where they could see the carnage, and had kept their word; our gentlemen ought to do the same.

Virginians always speak of their soldiers and of ours (when within our lines) as gentlemen. We say men, sometimes in the country regiments "boys," and it has a curious effect to hear a lady say "That gentleman has killed one of my sheep;" the property claim makes the title paradoxical. When we were not near, in the freedom of the social circle we were commonly called "Yanks," and the smallest children have confessed that their infant tongues were taught to prefix naughty words to that contemptuous title. But on this occasion circumstances had made us gentlemen *pro tem.*, so we gave our knightly words of honor not to bring red war to the door-step of the Dinwiddie Hotel, and then betook ourselves to merry song, and harmony ruled the hour.

During the night the rain gave out, doubtless fatigued with constant falling, and very early on the 31st we were in the saddle, riding along the lines to learn if the enemy was making any demonstration, and to send out reconnoissances if all was quiet.

Notwithstanding the fact that Dinwiddie Court House was not a paying locality for a hotel, and of no great account as a town, it was of considerable importance in a military point of view. It is a hub from which no end of roads diverge. The Boydton Plank Road passes by on the way to Petersburg, and led to the left flank of the Army of the Potomac, which stretched across it trying to reach the White Oak Road; then there is the Five Forks Road, with its ramifications, and a smaller road to the left of that which crosses Chamberlaine's Bed or Run, and runs on in the direction of the White Oak Road. On the other hand, there are as many avenues leading away toward the James River, which we were compelled to cover and protect. The suddenness of our first move had given us possession of Dinwiddie Court House, and now the enemy, appreciating the importance of the position, evidently proposed to secure the advantages which we were enjoying there; that is the military advantages—not the piano and the ladies. We have done with them for the present. But—

"If our voices come back, and we don't get shot,
We'll come back with them—otherwise not."

It soon became evident that the enemy was restless, from the pattering shot dropping here and there on the dull, damp air of the morning, and we had not long to wait before he determined as to our weak point, and came down upon it like a battering-ram, according to his headlong habit.

Beyond Dinwiddie Court House, looking north, the ground is high, and tolerably clear and level for a hundred yards or more, and then slopes down toward Chamberlaine's Bed, which is curtained with woods. The road that crosses the bed was held by Smith's brigade, of Crook's division, on the extreme left of our line, and here the enemy made their first assault, about ten o'clock in the morning. They came on fiercely, and some of them got on to our side of the water, but the brigade met them with a very determined resistance, and they were slowly driven back across the run, our men halting only when they had reached the bank. Meanwhile our bands played on the hill, and entertained the combatants with gay and patriotic airs.

To the right of Smith General Irvine Gregg was posted, in the low ground along the bed, and on his right was General Davies's brigade, with his right flank joining the left of the first division, which had already moved out as far as Five Forks, but, encountering a strong body of infantry, had been forced to retire, and now circled across the Five Forks Road toward the Boydton Plank. Somewhere in this line the enemy's cavalry hoped to find a gap or make one; and after wasting the better half of the morning in the vain assault on Smith, and in ill-tempered firing across the bed after their repulse, they moved slowly up the run, looked in upon Irvine Gregg, whose fine brigade, protected by a marsh, could laugh at them, and passing him, found both a better piece of country for their designs, and prospect of success, in front of General Davies. Heavily reinforced by infantry from the White Oak Road, they attacked him fiercely, and elbowed him out of his place in line, and crowded him back upon the two brigades of the first division under Devin, upon his right. Mounted and dismounted, as the ground permitted, these troops then together contested every grove and every knoll, and fell back slowly toward the Boydton Plank Road before the overpowering force of the enemy.

If this has been clearly understood, it will be seen that our line was now broken in two, all on the right of the Five Forks Road (looking toward that point) having been swept off in the direction of the Army of the Potomac, with the enemy between them and our troops on the left of that road; and now, in following the retiring lines of Davies and Devin, the enemy bore to the right, with the double object of entirely cutting off all communication between the divided sections of our command, and thus, while gaining possession of the Boydton Plank Road, force the troops on the left of our line to abandon Dinwiddie Court House.

Fortunately General Gibbes, with the reserve brigade which had been held in hand for emergencies, was standing to horse where the Five Forks Road is intersected by a dirt road that runs off to the Boydton Plank, about a mile above Dinwiddie. As the marching flank of the enemy in pursuit of Davies and Devin, wheeling toward the Plank Road, came crashing through the woods, General Gibbes was ordered to attack, and his gallant brigade had hardly started before they struck the enemy in flank and rear. Almost simultaneously with General Gibbes's assault, General Irvine Gregg was ordered to leave his position on Chamberlaine's Run, move rapidly by his right flank, mounted, and taking a wood-path leading over to the Five Forks Road, fall upon the enemy's rear on the left of General Gibbes. This order was promptly executed, and the sudden and combined attack thus made by these brigades caused the enemy to face about by the rear rank and look to his own defense. Davies and Devin were thus at once relieved of the pressure of the enemy's pursuit, and the trouble was averted that must have resulted from the appearance of this force in rear of the left flank of the Army of the Potomac, toward which they had been retreating.

The result of the movements just described having been anticipated, General Davies had been already instructed, through General Merritt, to bring his command, with Devin's division, to Dinwiddie Court House, by way of the Boydton Plank Road, which had not yet fallen into possession of the enemy.

It would have been possible at this time, as the enemy turned to meet the attack of Gibbes and Irvine Gregg, for Davies and Devin to have complicated his affairs somewhat by advancing upon his line as soon as he ceased to follow them; but it is easy to image that their commands were in rather an unavailable shape for offensive purposes after the severe retreating fight in which they had borne themselves so gallantly. Owing to the woody nature of the country, too, it was impossible for them to comprehend the exact position of the enemy in relation to our troops upon the left, and they could not therefore, perhaps, have been expected to do more than get together their men and horses, and march to Dinwiddie Court House as rapidly as possible. This they did, but only rejoined the command after the fighting was over for the day. No disaster resulted from want of their troops, however, as our men upon the left proved equal to the emergency which they were compelled to meet, when the enemy, quickly recovering from the shock of the unexpected attack in rear, assumed the offensive in that direction, and, with their largely superior force, pressed back the brigades of Gibbes and Gregg toward Dinwiddie Court House.

It was evident now that we had a difficult matter in hand, requiring the most careful attention and delicate management if we proposed to quarter in the Dinwiddie Hotel that evening. General Sheridan did so propose; and while throwing into the conflict in front all his energies, roused now to the highest pitch by the enemy's success, he sent off rapid riders to General Custer, in rear, who had been laboring all this time with the wagons and had not reached Dinwiddie, and ordered him to bring two of his brigades quickly to the front. Custer never required more than simple orders on such an occasion, for he had in himself the vim which insured a prompt response to the wishes of the commanding general; and so, forsaking the uncongenial task to which he had been a martyr, he hurried forward at the head of these brigades, and reported to General Sheridan at a critical moment when this excellent reinforcement was sorely needed.

The enemy, in attacking Gibbes and Gregg, had not only reversed their ranks, but, in order to protect themselves from troops that we might have on the left of Gregg, had necessarily changed the direction of their march, and now the fight gradually crept along toward Chamberlaine's Bed, on which they sought to rest their right flank, to secure themselves from further surprise. This backward movement delayed them somewhat, of course, and favored us also, in the fact that, by swinging round in that direction they relieved both Gibbes and Gregg, who had been hard pushed, and found fresh opponents in the fine brigade of General Smith, which now disputed warmly their approach along the bed. It was just as the carbines of Smith began to rattle in the woods below that the head of Custer's column reached the high ground in front of Dinwiddie Court House.

On the right of this open ridge the brigades of Gibbes and Gregg were seen slowly retiring and forming in line again, covering the Boydton Plank Road. Along the edge of the woods in their front, the gray uniforms of the rebel infantry could be distinguished moving off toward Smith, and evidently bent upon ousting him from his position on the bed before they attempted anything further. Seeing this, Gibbes's brigade, on our extreme right, moved forward again with spirit, and kept the enemy in its front diverted, while Smith continued his splendid effort against the large force now attacking him. General Sheridan instructed General Smith that when compelled to retire, as every one saw he must do, he should fall back to the high, open ground in rear, and go into position on the extreme left of the line, which we were now preparing to defend to the last. The first brigade of Custer's division was dismounted on the hill, and immediately set to work with a will to throw up a breast-work of rails, and the neighboring fences were rapidly sacrificed for the purpose.

Now, for almost the first time during this hard day's fight, could artillery be used, and the horse batteries went quickly into position and awaited the coming enemy. Smith held on to the bed with tight-clinched hands, and only let go his hold when he had hardly a round of ammunition left; then, abandoning the road on which he had been fighting, he took to the woods in front of our left, and trudged up the hill toward Dinwiddie, unmolested.

At this moment the enemy's cavalry appeared upon the stage in one short act. Apparently they had been formed on the west bank of the bed, and now, as Smith abandoned the road, these fiery cavaliers dashed over the bed, and galloped wildly up the slope to cut off Smith, to get possession of the Court House, to salute the ladies, and be patted on the back; and as a staff officer, who had just left General Smith, was telling General Sheridan that he was taking to the woods on our left and front, the enemy's cavalry rode suddenly into the open ground below us. But by this time Irvine Gregg and Custer's brigade were snugly fortified on the crest, calmly awaiting the progress of events. It seemed impossible that the enemy should have so soon gained the road from which the smoke of Smith's carbines had not yet cleared away, and for a moment our troops hesitated to fire, but only for an instant, and then they poured in a scathing volley upon the astonished column, which had staggered with surprise when it first emerged from the woods, and had halted in a mass, huddled together by the weight of its own impetus. The hot fire that burst out now from our breastworks seemed to wither this rash cavalry, for it vanished from sight, and was seen no more that day.

The sun was nearly down now, but one more effort of the enemy was yet to be made to get possession of Dinwiddie Court House, and win some fruits of the hard day's work, which, so far, had borne but barren honor. The thundering salute to their cavalry had hardly ceased to echo through the woods when the long line of their infantry slowly debouched on the plain—

infantry that was hard to beat. We used to think that living was such a poor life with them that they did not much care to continue it. They had an air of *abandon*, a sort of devil-may-care swing in their long stride as they advanced over a field, that was rather disheartening to men that did not want to get shot. And these were some of their best—parts or all of Pickett's and Johnson's divisions of Anderson's corps. While they were still deploying, Pennington's brigade of Custer's division reached the field, and was immediately ordered to the right, to the support of Gibbes. Catching sight of the enemy, Pennington's men burst into a glorious cheer as they splashed through the miry road behind the rails, and from left to right the shout was passed along, while General Sheridan, cap in hand, galloped up the line with some of his staff and Generals Merritt and Custer, who were with him at the moment, and drew the first fire of the now advancing enemy. Mud and bullets flew, and an enthusiastic reporter of the *New York Herald*, who was carried away by his feelings at this juncture, was shot in the shoulder following the general. Our artillery now opened, and at such short range could not fail to be destructive, and a moment later the carbines of five brigades were blazing in the twilight, the repeating Spensers puffing out their cartridges like Roman candles. The heavy fire from both sides continued for a few minutes, and, meanwhile, darkness settled down upon us. Gradually the fire from the enemy became fitful and irregular, and soon ceased altogether, for, as they advanced across the open ground, they seemed to count the cost of carrying our line, and weigh the advantages of holding the Court House by such uncertain tenure as theirs would be, separated by miles from their own army, and liable to be annihilated before they could rejoin it. Acting on the conclusion of this sober second thought, they contented themselves with such glory as the day had brought, and, wrapping themselves up in it, lay down in their tracks to rest as soon as the slacking of our fire permitted.

Thus closed one of the severest and best of our cavalry fights; one that tested to the extreme the endurance and the spirit of the command, and proved again its gallantry and steadfastness. The fight did not close with a grand *feu-de-joie* or a blaze of glory. It flickered, and then went out, because the enemy, who might have made it dramatic, decided to have it commonplace, and we appreciated his motives too well to attempt to have it otherwise, for we would, unquestionably, have been roughly handled had we mistaken his hesitancy and sallied out of our breast-works to attack him. We felt entitled to some glory too, at nightfall, for if the enemy's object was to gain possession of Dinwiddie Court House, we had foiled him in that; if he had intended to cripple our cavalry and prevent our acting against his right and rear, he had failed in that, as he discovered next morning; and if his only object was a fight, he had got a Roland for his Oliver, and he had captured no prisoners and no material of war. It was hard to see wherein he had bettered himself, or disproportionately damaged us, so we did not feel downhearted; though we had lost some ground, we still held the key that opened the way to the enemy's right and rear, and our own communications were all intact, and we still kept the Dinwiddie Hotel.

In his official report General Grant says that in this battle of Dinwiddie Court House General Sheridan displayed great generalship, and the lieutenant-general is good authority. It is hoped that the reader has been able to see how the general displayed generalship: in extricating his command from the complications in which it was involved by the difficult nature of the country and the superior strength of the enemy; in keeping employed this formidable force, which might have caused infinite annoyance to the left flank of the Army of the Potomac; and at the same time retaining his hold of the strategic point from which new efforts could best be made, and where his presence was a standing threat to the enemy's communications.

When it became evident that the enemy had no intention of making any further demonstration, General Sheridan retired to a small house in rear of our lines, and sent off a dispatch to the lieutenant-general briefly narrating the events of the day, and adding, for his information, that the force of the enemy was too strong for us, left him to take such action as he might deem proper, while assuring him that our command would not leave Dinwiddie until compelled to do so. The dispatch reads as follows:

CAVALRY HEADQUARTERS,
DINWIDDIE COURT HOUSE,
March 31st, 1865.

LIEUTENANT-GENERAL GRANT,
 Commanding Armies of the United States:

The enemy's cavalry attacked me about ten o'clock to-day, on the road coming in from the west, and a little north of Dinwiddie Court House. This attack was handsomely repulsed by General Smith's brigade, of Crook's division, and the enemy was driven across Chamberlaine's Creek. Shortly afterward the enemy's infantry attacked on the same creek in heavy force, and drove in General Davies's brigade, and advancing rapidly, gained the forks of the road at J. Boisseau's. This forced Devin, who was in advance, and Davies to cross to the Boydton Road. General Gregg's brigade and General Gibbes's brigade, which had been toward Dinwiddie, then attacked the enemy in the rear very handsomely. This stopped the march toward the left of our infantry, and finally caused them to turn toward

Dinwiddie and attack us in heavy force. The enemy then again attacked at Chamberlaine's Creek, and forced Smith's position. At this time Capehart's and Pennington's brigades, of Custer's division, came up, and a very handsome fight occurred. The enemy have gained some ground, but we still hold in front of Dinwiddie, and Davies and Devin are coming down the Boydton Road to join us. The opposing force was Pickett's division: Wise's independent brigade of infantry, and Fitzhugh Lee's, Rosser's, and W. H. Lee's cavalry commands. The men behaved splendidly. Our loss in killed and wounded will probably number four hundred and fifty men; very few were lost as prisoners. We have of the enemy a number of prisoners. This force is too strong for us. I will hold out at Dinwiddie Court House until I am compelled to leave. Our fighting to-day was all dismounted.

(Signed)   P. H. SHERIDAN,
Major-General.

The house where this was written was a poor frame affair, inhabited by a woman and a half-dozen little children, who were living on Heaven knows what in that desert land; their house filled with wounded, and a fear of having it riddled with shot in the morning. It was a relief to get away from it and put Davies's and Devin's troops into camp behind Dinwiddie Court House as they marched into our lines by way of the Boydton Plank Road. By midnight every preparation for the morning was completed: ammunition was brought up and distributed; wagons were parked at the point they had reached, some three or four miles still short of Dinwiddie; the wounded were all cared for and moved to the rear; and then we betook ourselves again to the hotel, where we fell down on the softest board that offered, and were asleep.

Meanwhile the lieutenant-general seems to have been awake, as we find that he immediately acted upon General Sheridan's report of the fight at Dinwiddie by ordering to his support MacKenzie's division of cavalry from the Army of the James, and first one division and then the whole of the Fifth Corps. General Grant evidently deemed it important that General Sheridan should not be foiled in his effort to break through the enemy's right flank, and therefore sent to him a force sufficient to accomplish that end—a judicious reinforcement, that led to the best results.

Unfortunately, however, there is associated with the brilliant operations which followed an unpleasant personal matter, which ought perhaps to be noticed here. Everybody will remember that at the battle of Five Forks, on April 1st, Major-General Warren was relieved from the command of the Fifth Army Corps by General

Sheridan, and ordered to report to General Grant, and as we are on the eve of that engagement, it seems proper to speak of this incident now, because General Sheridan was undoubtedly influenced to his action in regard to General Warren partially by events preceding the battle. At the time much interest was felt in the community to learn the real causes of General Warren's removal, for he was an officer of prominence in the Army of the Potomac, and his record and reputation were such that it is a question whether this personal affair did not cause as much discussion in the North as the important battle of which it was an incident. This interest has been kept alive by supporters of the two officers concerned; and lately, if the circumstance was in danger of being forgotten, attention has again been called to it by the pamphlet of General Warren, giving his version of the difficulty, interwoven with a sketch of the operations of his corps. In view of these circumstances it would be idle to ignore this subject in a narrative purporting to follow General Sheridan through this campaign, and as the steps by which he finally reached his determination to relieve General Warren lead through the whole of this day's operations, the reader will doubtless prefer to take them in turn, as thus he will be better able to decide whether General Sheridan was justified in this summary action toward a fellow-officer at the close of a successful day.

In discussing this question a sincere endeavor will be made to treat it fairly and impartially; because, in the first place, General Sheridan does not need to have his reputation upheld at the expense of any other officer, and because good taste and truth would alike condemn a blind panegyric which facts do not support. No reader can fail to appreciate General Warren's delicate position; but in General Sheridan's behalf it is needful to discuss some portions of General Warren's pamphlet, and the reader is only asked to draw his own conclusions from the records from which we quote. Some influential newspapers have decided this case already in favor of General Warren without hearing the other side, looking at the controversy from his stand-point; but it is believed that the facts can be shown to sustain General Sheridan, looking at the matter from neutral ground. It may be well to add, that if this sketch here and there smacks of defense, it is only because in some points at issue General Sheridan cannot well make himself heard, and therefore it seems simple justice to lay before the reader what can with propriety be advanced in his behalf; and as the events which we are describing will some day be studied by the historian, whose task is an unenviable one at best, the testimony of eye-witnesses will always be valuable provided it be true.

We have seen that General Grant acted at

once upon General Sheridan's dispatch from Dinwiddie, and then he wrote a note to him as follows:

DABNEY MILLS,
March 31st, 1865, 10.05 P.M.

MAJOR-GENERAL SHERIDAN:

The Fifth Corps has been ordered to your support. Two divisions will go by J. Boisseau's and one down the Boydton Road. In addition to this I have sent MacKenzie's cavalry, which will reach you by the Vaughan Road. All these forces, except the cavalry, should reach you by twelve o'clock to-night. You will assume command of the whole force sent to operate with you, and use it to the best of your ability to destroy the force which your command has fought so gallantly to-day.

(Signed) U. S. GRANT,
Lieutenant-General.

This is all that passed on the subject between General Sheridan and the lieutenant-general. It is short and to the point on both sides, especially that part regarding reinforcements—quite a model of military correspondence; and the action of the lieutenant-general, unquestioning and uncomplaining, evinces a confidence that must have been gratifying to his lieutenant at Dinwiddie. General Grant says, speaking of the Fifth Corps, "Two divisions will go by J. Boisseau's and one down the Boydton Road, and should reach you by twelve o'clock to-night." Here begins the association of General Warren with General Sheridan, and so, with the reader's permission, we will now change the scene to the camp of the Fifth Corps, on the left of the Army of the Potomac.

CHAPTER V.

A FIGHT ABOUT FIVE FORKS.

On the morning of the 31st of March the force of the enemy which afterward attacked our cavalry in front of Dinwiddie had dealt rather roughly with General Warren's command, and repulsed his effort to gain the White Oak Road. It is not important to refer to this except that the lieutenant-general's report speaks disparagingly of General Warren in connection with this affair, which doubtless influenced the action of both these officers in the events of the following day. When the enemy had withdrawn from his front General Warren pushed up, and took possession of the White Oak Road, just where the right of Lee's fortified line protecting Petersburg ends, three or four miles to the east of Five Forks, and in the rear, of course, of the enemy's troops at Dinwiddie, which, it will be seen, were thus cut off from the main body of their army. While carrying on this operation on their own account, General Grant wished to take advantage of their adventurous isolation to throw the Fifth Corps upon them and annihilate them. To carry out this design, General Warren was ordered, through General Meade, to move his command as stated in the dispatch of the lieutenant-general to General Sheridan; the movement by the Boydton Plank Road being against the enemy's flank, and that by Boisseau's house directly upon their rear.

It would be tedious to follow the course of General Warren's narrative of the obstacles he encountered in attempting to comply with this order, and the civilian reader will be glad to be spared a full discussion as to whether they might have been overcome; but some of the difficulties he found seem almost incompatible with the condition of active warfare in which we were supposed to be. Fancy, for instance, a command so near to the enemy that it "could not be roused by drums or bugle calls, or loud commands, with safety," and yet which could not be roused by other means in less than an hour and a half! Fancy critical movements expected at any moment—the enemy within earshot, and a corps, lying on its arms, only to be set on foot with such rapidity as this: "Supposing all possible dispatch used, twenty minutes at least would be required for me to make the necessary arrangements; twenty minutes more would be required to carry my orders to the divisions; twenty more minutes for them to transmit them to the brigades; and forty minutes at least for the troops to get ready to move."(!) The civilian might well demand "Why does not the Army of the Potomac move?" if a corps commander replies that it takes two hours to wake the men when the enemy can hear the word of command. We could beat that in the cavalry, and wake the horses too.

Other difficulties presented themselves on the roads leading to Dinwiddie by which General Warren was directed to march. Gravelly Run crosses the Boydton Plank Road between Dinwiddie and General Warren's position, and the bridge over the run was broken, and General Warren complains that this was not taken into account in forming the expectations for his prompt reinforcement of General Sheridan by that road, and especially finds fault with General Sheridan for ignoring this impediment, in speaking of the slow movements, in his official report, and with General Grant for authorizing its publication, for, as General Warren says, "this route was used for communications between General Grant and General Sheridan." That is very true. The staff officer who carried the dispatches before alluded to, on this same evening had gone that way, and his horse had forded Gravelly Run at the bridge without wetting his rider's boots; the bottom of the run was hard as a rock, and there was no current to speak of. The bad weather and the bad roads had already soiled the clothes and shoes of General Warren's men, and they were as wet already as water and mud could make them; and it is not too much to say that a little enterprise would have overcome this obstacle, for the practicability of the ford could have been tested by riding a horse into it as General Sheridan's staff officer did. On the other road, leading to the enemy's rear by J. Boisseau's house, of which General Grant speaks, no effort was made to march until after daylight, and therefore it is not worth while to speculate as to what force of the enemy might have been encountered there. General Warren's whole action in regard to the reinforcement by this road is quite incomprehensible. In the first place, when fearing that the proposed contraction of the lines of the Army of the Potomac on this night would affect the morale of the troops as indicating a failure, he had, in the most praiseworthy manner, himself proposed to General Meade to move exactly as he was subsequently directed to do, for the purpose of falling upon the rear of the enemy confronting General Sheridan; but when ordered to do this his feet seemed entangled in a mesh. By that road, too, the troops would have to cross Gravelly Run, but, though here was no difficulty of fording, a staff officer had reported long lines of camp fires, and much chopping of wood, and other indications of the presence of the foe upon the lower bank, and this report so influenced General Warren that he came to the determination, notwithstanding the most urgent dispatches from General Meade, to keep these two divisions where they were until he could hear that General Ayres, who had gone to Dinwiddie by the Boydton Plank Road with the other division, had certainly reinforced General Sheridan. General Meade wrote: "A dispatch partially transmitted is received, indicating the bridge over Gravelly Run is destroyed, and time will be required to rebuild it. If this is the case, would not time be gained by sending the troops by the Quaker Road? Time is of the utmost importance. Sheridan cannot maintain himself at Dinwiddie without reinforcements, and yours are the only ones that can be sent. Use every exertion to get troops to him as soon as possible. If necessary, send troops by both roads, and give up the rear attack. If Sheridan is not reinforced and compelled to fall back, he will retire by the Vaughan Road."

General Warren seems to misapprehend the spirit of this dispatch, and to consider that General Meade's urgency was because of a general solicitude for General Sheridan's position, and not directed to him at all. Some reader may fancy that so pressing an order was intended to start the tardy column of General Warren, and impress him with the importance of utmost haste. It reads so. It seems to say, "stand not upon the order of your going, but go at once! Hurry! If you reinforce General Sheridan he can hold his ground, if not, he may be obliged to retreat." But General Warren, calmly ignoring General Meade and the emergency that was so earnestly set before him, decided that he would not reinforce General Sheridan; that not being reinforced he would retreat, and that his retreating would cause such a condition of things as would render the presence of his own command desirable where it then was; and he justifies this decision by the successful battle of the following day, which probably would not have happened exactly as it did if all the other things had not happened exactly as they did. Perhaps so; but then it is possible that a good deal of cavalry fighting before the battle of Five Forks might have been dispensed with, and a good deal of the hard fighting of the day might have been avoided, if General Warren had swept down upon the enemy's rear at daylight that morning, as he was expected and ordered to do. One supposition is as reasonable as the other.

Another point in dispute is as to whether the enemy remained until daylight in front of General Sheridan or fell back to Five Forks during the night. General Warren thinks they did fall back, General Sheridan thinks they did not. The former bases his opinion upon the reports of deserters, the latter upon what he saw. General Ayres, who commanded the division of the Fifth Corps which reinforced General Sheridan by way of the Boydton Plank Road, after rebuilding the bridge across Gravelly Run, says, "as we approached, just after daylight, the enemy hastily decamped;" and General Warren, in his pamphlet, unintentionally, no doubt, perverts this report by saying, "They had withdrawn in the night, carrying off their wounded, and leaving only a cavalry picket in General Sheridan's front, which, as General Ayres says, hastily decamped,"—which General Ayres does not say. He says, "*the enemy* hastily decamped;" and in regard to this force of the enemy General Sheridan officially reports, "I moved my cavalry force at daylight against the enemy's lines in front, which gave way rapidly, moving off by the right flank, and crossing Chamberlaine's Creek." The cavalry pickets of the enemy were never spoken of as their "lines." Again, he says, "As they fell back the enemy were rapidly followed by General Merritt's two divisions. * * * I then determined that I would drive the enemy with the cavalry to Five Forks. * * * Meantime General Merritt's command continued to press the enemy, and by impetuous charges drove them from two lines of temporary works," which could not have occurred had the enemy withdrawn to Five Forks during the night. General Warren, while imputing ignorance of the actual state of affairs to the lieutenant-general and to General Meade, seems again to misapprehend the spirit of his orders when he says, "To join General Sheridan by midnight on this route, I then had to capture or destroy whatever of this force was between me and General Sheridan." At 10.15 P.M. General Meade had ordered him to move by this route with the two divisions of which General Grant speaks, and attack the enemy, and took care to point out his course in case the enemy should turn upon him, so that if he did not succeed in reaching General Sheridan, according to the expectations of General Grant, his failure was provided for; and there seems to be no good reason why he should not have made the attempt. He met with no opposition when he did make it, and he claims that there was no enemy there at all. Meanwhile he could have communicated with General Sheridan by way of the Boydton Plank Road, as General Sheridan did so communicate with him in a dispatch dated 3 A.M., on April 1st, which he sent off, in his anxiety lest the plans for the attack should not be fully understood and consummated. He wrote, "I understand you have a division at J. Boisseau's, if so, you are in rear of the enemy's line, and almost on his flank. I will hold on here. Possibly they may attack Custer at daylight, if so, attack instantly and in full force; attack at daylight anyhow," etc. This understanding of General Warren's position turned out to be a misunderstanding, but it was based upon General Grant's dispatch and General Sheridan's own expectations—reasonable enough we may presume, from the fact that General Warren made no effort then to prove them unreasonable. If he had moved, as ordered by

General Meade, and encountered formidable opposition, no fault could have been found, and had he failed to reinforce General Sheridan, doubtless the battle of Five Forks would have been fought all the same, for the enemy would unquestionably have made the same futile and blundering effort to hold that point for the protection of the Southside Railroad.

So much for the disappointments of the morning; we shall see that when General Grant heard of them he was not pleased.

Meanwhile, before daybreak, General Sheridan and his staff might have been very indistinctly seen emerging from the Dinwiddie Hotel and mounting their trusty steeds. It was a very foggy morning; even after the hour of sunrise heavy vapors rendered only indistinctness perceptible, and when we reached the picket-line of Custer's division, which was in front, beyond Dinwiddie, the most straining eyes could not see many yards beyond the works which our men had strengthened during the night, and were now fit to resist horse, foot, or dragoons. Gradually the fog lifted, and Generals Sheridan, Merritt, and Custer, each with staff and escort, proceeded to make a reconnoissance which soon developed a long line of infantry, with skirmishers to the front, and mounted officers prancing gayly about. The question then arose under which king this line was marshaled. We had heard nothing of the Fifth Corps, which was to attack at daylight, and it seemed very possible that the enemy might have stolen away in the night, declining to be sandwiched between General Warren's command and our cavalry, and this, then, might be the Fifth Corps confronting us. There was a great division of opinion. Field-glasses were leveled and eyes were shaded to discover whether the line was friend or foe. Some cried "they're blue!" and some "they're gray!" but for awhile nobody was sufficiently certain to venture any nearer; already we were within easy musket range, but not a shot was fired—still the line did not advance, neither did it retire, and the anxiety for some sort of demonstration was growing painful, when one of Custer's staff discovered, through his glass, most unmistakable blue, and dashed boldly down toward a mounted officer who was caracoling his horse on the neutral ground between our party and his skirmishers. We heard a "Halt!" a question and an answer, and then the sharp report of a pistol, and Custer's officer came galloping back through the muddy field, and was able to report positively that the line was gray—a very gray gentleman having shot at him and called him some highly improper names. Our cavalry was at once ordered forward, and while the order was being carried back to the troops the stolid line faced to the right and coiled itself rapidly into the woods, only giving us time to send after it our compliments in a couple of rifled shells, which were fired partly for the sake of the damage they might do, but principally as a signal to General Warren that we were on the move, with the enemy in front of us. But as he had hardly yet started from his last night's encampment, we might well have saved the ammunition.

At the point where General Gibbes's brigade on the preceding day had so handsomely attacked the enemy in flank as they pressed after General Davies, we met the head of General Ayres's division, of the Fifth Corps, which had come by way of the Boydton Plank Road, and here it was that General Ayres caught sight of the enemy as they "hastily decamped" across Chamberlaine's Bed. There were no tidings yet of the two other divisions which were to come by way of Boisseau's house, and as General Ayres's men were fatigued with marching and loss of their night's rest, General Sheridan directed that they should be massed where they were, cook their coffee, get their breakfast, and await further orders. The skirmishers of the cavalry had already overtaken the enemy's rear-guard, and there was lively shooting going on in the tangled woods, through which the advance of our mounted men was penetrating as well as it could, while the main column of the cavalry, under General Merritt, moved up the Five Forks Road. General Sheridan then sent a staff officer, with a squadron, to communicate, if possible, with General Warren by way of J. Boisseau's house, and learn what delayed him, and when he might be expected to arrive. Just in front of the historical Mr. Boisseau's (who must pardon to the truth of history the liberties taken with his name) this party met General Griffin at the head of his division of the Fifth Corps. It was now between seven and eight o'clock, and the slippery enemy had slipped across Chamberlaine's Bed, and were throwing up a little line of works to check the progress of our cavalry. General Warren, with Crawford's division of his corps, had not yet come up, but was engaged in making a tactical retreat from his old position on the White Oak Road. His precautions were not necessary though, for the enemy took no notice of his withdrawal—"an oversight," says General Warren, "not to have been expected from our previous experience;" and it is well to note this here, for, as General Warren's subsequent removal from the command of his corps seems to have been more due to his skeptical mood in regard to success than to any positive delinquency, we may find in these words some indication of his feeling in regard to the enemy's generalship, and how it affected his mind.

Seeing that the slow progress of these two divisions would render their prompt co-operation with the cavalry impracticable, General Sheridan directed General Griffin to mass his command at Boisseau's, and get coffee and breakfast, and wait further orders; and then General Merritt was instructed to press on after the enemy, and, if possible, drive them into their fortified lines at Five Forks, where General Sheridan anticipated they would remain, and where he thought they could be attacked to great advantage by the combined force of his cavalry and infantry. Meanwhile General Crook was ordered to keep his division in hand in front of Dinwiddie Court House, and watch the crossings of Chamberlaine's Bed.

Merritt pushed on in his usual energetic manner, and was soon pretty heavily engaged, the enemy availing himself of every favorable piece of ground to hold our men in check, and yet, when our lines were formed and ready to attack, would generally move rapidly off again, his infantry gliding through the woods with ease, while our cavalry labored hard in pursuit through the thick undergrowth and miry soil. Twice the enemy took time to throw up temporary breast-works, and endeavored to hold them with a portion of their troops, but General Merritt dismounted part of his command and quickly drove them out. It is a section of country more difficult for cavalry operations than it is possible to imagine: the fields all quicksands, the woods all jungle; and there were heavy casualties among Merritt's men, for which General Sheridan hoped soon to compensate by an important success. At 2 P.M. the last of the enemy had retired behind the works at Five Forks, along the White Oak Road, and General Merritt had pressed up so close that their skirmish line was drawn in, and they evidently awaited a general attack.

Meanwhile Crawford's division, of the Fifth Corps, had joined General Griffin, and about 11 A.M. General Warren reported to General Sheridan, and says that "his manner was cordial and friendly." General Sheridan had hours before given up all hope of doing anything in front of Dinwiddie Court House in co-operation with General Warren's command, and his disappointment of the morning was now forgotten in his designs for the attack at Five Forks. He is not the man to waste time in lamenting his own spilled milk while there is an enemy at hand whose milk is yet to be spilled. General MacKenzie's division of cavalry, from the Army of the James, which had been sent by General Grant as an additional reinforcement, and is spoken of in his dispatch, arrived at Dinwiddie Court House about this time, and was ordered by General Sheridan to remain near that point until its services should be required. This was a division only in name; in point of numbers it was not a brigade, barely one thousand men, but good employment was found for them, and MacKenzie with a small division is better than some older officers with a big one.

About 1 P.M.—as soon as it was evident that

the enemy would retire to his fortified line at Five Forks before accepting battle—orders were sent to General Warren to bring up his corps, and Major Gillespie, of the engineers, was instructed by General Sheridan as to the position it should occupy on the Gravelly Church Road— a little lane running across from the White Oak to the Five Forks Road, something like a mile from the Forks, toward Petersburg, off on the right and rear of Merritt's cavalry, and opposite the enemy's left flank. The formation was directed to be made obliquely to the White Oak Road—that is, the right of the corps to be nearest to the road, the object being to burst upon the enemy's left flank upon that road, and to waste no time in unnecessary marching in doing so. Had the corps been formed exactly parallel to the road, it will be seen that the right of the corps, in order to strike the enemy's left flank, would, after crossing the road, have to make a complete left wheel, in which much time would be lost, and, meanwhile, the brunt of the fighting would have to be borne by the left of the line, which, having the shortest distance to wheel, would naturally encounter the enemy first. Hence the oblique formation, in which it was supposed that the right of the line would strike the enemy as soon as the left or center. Two divisions constituted the front line, and the other division supported the right. In regard to this formation General Warren remarks: "General Sheridan says in his report that he directed one division to be formed in reserve, opposite the center. This is a mistake; his order was to form it in rear of the right." If General Warren had read the report more carefully he would have observed that General Sheridan says this in speaking of his instructions to Major Gillespie, given before he had himself seen the ground, and he would have found a few lines later these words: "I ordered an advance in the following formation: Ayres's division on the left, in double lines, and Crawford's division on the right, in double lines, and Griffin's division in reserve, behind Crawford;" that is, in rear of the right, as General Warren says, and General Sheridan appears not to have made a mistake if we read all that *he* says.

During this formation, which was slowly perfected, General Merritt was instructed to keep up a lively fire along his front, protecting his men as much as possible by such shelter as the ground afforded while engaging the attention of the enemy; and General Warren sent his mounted escort up to the open ground overlooking the White Oak Road, to picket his front while his corps was getting into position. But the enemy seemed to have no idea of coming events, or were wonderfully indifferent if they had, for they made no effort to look into our little game on Gravelly Run, but seemed satisfied to "go it blind" behind their fortifications.

It was now reported that some movements on the left of the Army of the Potomac had left open the White Oak Road by which General Lee might yet reinforce the isolated Five Forks party if he felt so disposed; and already some small force of the enemy was said to be reconnoitering this road from the direction of Petersburg. Meantime MacKenzie's cavalry had been moved up to Mr. Boisseau's house, and was therefore in good position to reach the White Oak Road rapidly by the way the Fifth Corps had come in the morning, and learn the truth of these reports. This he was ordered to do, and to attack with vigor whatever he should meet, as it was of vital importance that no disturbing element should now intrude upon the ripening plans for a decisive battle. He was ordered to drive toward Petersburg, if possible, whatever force he might encounter, and, if successful, to return quickly along the White Oak Road toward Five Forks, and take part in the flank attack. If he encountered nothing, he was ordered to pursue his reconnoissance only so far as to ascertain that the Fifth Corps would not be attacked from that direction, and then return as above detailed. If he met a superior force, he was to hold it in check as best he might; but hold it in check he must at all hazards. Enterprising MacKenzie rode gayly away on this three-cornered errand, while the Fifth Corps plodded through the mud and formed on Gravelly Run.

After General Sheridan had seen the cavalry close up to the enemy's works, and had talked the plan over till Merritt had it by heart, he struck across toward Gravelly Church, and, dismounting from his horse on the bank of the run, impatiently awaited the formation of the Fifth Corps. Here began his dissatisfaction with General Warren in connection with this battle; he seemed so passive and indifferent in regard to the matter, that General Sheridan, repeatedly calling his attention to the importance of haste, could elicit no response beyond the urging of his division commanders through the medium of his staff. It was a time for active personal effort and example. It was growing late, and the days had gone by when the sun stood still in midheaven that enemies might be destroyed. But General Warren sat upon a log, and his indifferent manner he explains in this way. Speaking of General Sheridan, he says, "his impatience was no greater apparently than I felt myself, and which I strove to repress and prevent any exhibition of, as it would but tend to impair confidence in the proposed operations. When everything possible is being done, it is important to have the men think it is all that success requires if their confidence is to be retained." The reader can decide as to the merits of this argument. But it was most evident to all of us who knew General

Sheridan well, that he was much annoyed; and we remarked to each other that there would be a deuce of a row if the Fifth Corps was not ready to move out soon. He evidently considered that General Warren was throwing cold water on the proposed assault; and if he arrived at that conclusion, doubtless General Warren helped him to it by something more than an indifferent manner. What conversation they had upon the subject is nowhere officially recorded, and therefore is not fit matter for production here; but it is just to General Sheridan to say that General Warren did not seem to be hopeful, and gave all of us the impression of being unduly influenced by his belief in the sagacity of the enemy, who may have been never so sagacious, but this was not the time to dwell upon it. In his official report, General Sheridan himself declares: "In this connection I will say that General Warren did not exert himself to get up his corps as rapidly as he might have done, and his manner gave me the impression that he wished the sun to go down before dispositions for the attack could be completed." The reader will judge between the two, and decide for himself whether or not earnest hearty co-operation could have been so misunderstood, and whether the manner of an officer thoroughly believing in success, and impatient to realize it, would have required the explanation of apparent indifference which we have just cited.

About 4 P.M., all being in readiness at last, the order to advance was given, and the corps marched briskly forward across the miry bottom land that borders the Gravelly Run, through the undergrowth of brakes on the hill-side beyond, and quickly reached an open level plain, wider than our line of battle. Here we caught sight of the White Oak Road, some two hundred yards before us, and a little party of the enemy's cavalry moving restlessly about in the edge of the woods in our front. Across the plain the Fifth Corps moved magnificently, and General Sheridan with his staff and escort, and his beautiful headquarter flag, rode out between the skirmishers and the front line of battle, cantering from left to right, beaming with expectations of victory. His superb black horse "Rienzi," the same that Buchanan Read has immortalized in "Sheridan's Ride," plunged and curveted, whisking his broad tail, champing his bit, and tossing impatient flecks of foam in the air, as if he had caught the inspiration of the moment and was eager for the fray. Suddenly upon our right there emerged from the woods a column of cavalry rapidly pushing up the White Oak Road toward Five Forks, which some of the staff, galloping out to the front, soon made out to be the division of MacKenzie, who, in the execution of the orders we have already alluded to, had reached the White Oak Road by way of Boisseau's house, after a sharp little skirmish with some of the enemy's cavalry which he easily drove toward Petersburg; and countermarching promptly, in obedience to his instructions, now appeared upon our right just in time to participate in the general attack. Riding quickly across to General Sheridan, he was instructed to swing round with the right of the infantry and gain possession of the Ford Road, which leads from the Five Forks across Hatcher's Run, in the enemy's rear. With a cheery word for all of us, he galloped back to his command, and, turning the head of his column into the thick woods beyond the White Oak Road, steered the best course he could—guiding his movements by Crawford's division on the right of the Fifth Corps. Still pressing on, the infantry became somewhat engaged before they reached the White Oak Road; and just in front of the general one of our skirmishers threw up his arms and fell forward on to his face, as a man only does when he is shot through the heart. There was no show of force, though, and this was a parting shot from the restless cavalry, which now left the road and went back out of sight, no doubt to look after MacKenzie, as they couldn't hope to stop these heavy lines of infantry. Now we are almost on the White Oak Road, and it is important here to understand how the commanding general intended to bring these heavy lines to bear upon the enemy's left flank. General Warren says, "General Sheridan's calculation as to the position of the left flank of the enemy's line was faulty, and to a very serious extent," etc.; and he claims credit for rectifying this error by such prompt changes as the unexpected circumstances required. Let us look into this and see if the conception or the execution was at fault. General Warren's orders to his division commanders were as follows: "The line will move forward, as formed, till it reaches the White Oak Road, when it will swing round to the left, perpendicular to the White Oak Road;" that is, make a left wheel. The enemy's main line is simply the White Oak Road fortified upon the further side, and there is presumed to be a short line retired from this toward Hatcher's Run, to guard their left flank from surprise. This is the object of assault; this short line is to be quickly demolished before it can be heavily reinforced, and the cavalry are charged with keeping the main line busy by assaulting with vigor when they hear the musketry of the infantry attack. It has been already explained that the right of the corps was nearest to the White Oak Road—consequently it would naturally reach the road first, and begin first to wheel to the left. Crawford is on the right, supported by Griffin, and Ayres is on the left. If Crawford begins to wheel to his left as soon as he crosses the White Oak Road, he will be well on his way to the enemy's rear by the time Ayres reaches the road; and if Ayres shall encounter opposition, then Crawford and Griffin will be wrapping about the enemy like a cloak, and will soon demand attention. This is the conception, based upon supposed compliance with orders. Now, for the execution. Crawford on the right crossed the White Oak Road first, with but little opposition; but after crossing failed to wheel to his left, as ordered, and pushed straight on toward Hatcher's Run, where there was no enemy. That this serious mistake was made we will be able to prove by General Warren and by General Crawford himself. Meantime General Ayres, on the left, reached and crossed the White Oak Road, and was immediately received by a somewhat heavy fire upon his left flank, and, in accordance with his instructions, at once began to change front to the left. In speaking of General Sheridan's faulty calculations, General Warren says, "We were too far to our right of the enemy's left flank." Had we been farther to the left, General Ayres would have met a much heavier force, and would have found still greater difficulty in changing front. That the enemy was encountered here proves that he was found precisely where he was supposed to be; there was here no "unexpected condition of things," so far as the enemy was concerned, but it was entirely unexpected that Crawford should leave Ayres to deal with the enemy single-handed. Griffin naturally followed Crawford for awhile, being ordered to support him, but we shall see how handsomely he afterward came into the gap between Crawford and Ayres, and did good service there.

In reply to the fire which Ayres's men met, they opened a furious fusilade which shook the air and made the welkin ring again; but it was a spasmodic burst that probably did very little execution, for the enemy was not yet in sight, and was well protected by his works. Ayres's command had now entered the woods and could hardly see five yards ahead, and the men were nervous, not knowing what to expect behind the trees and brushes; and the greater part of one brigade soon grew very unsteady, though in this dreadful roar of musketry almost nobody on our side seemed to be killed as yet. One or two regiments broke and began to run. It was a sudden panic begotten of a hidden danger, and it was a moment when a little personal example and stiff swearing were badly needed. Fortunately General Sheridan happened to be at hand, and together with his staff rode into the ranks of the faltering troops, which were soon reassured, and taking heart again came back to their places in line. The opening fire of Ayres's division was immediately echoed along the White Oak Road by the carbines of Merritt's men, who gallantly responded to the preconcerted signal for assault, and now started boldly forward to perform their part. They had the brunt of the fight to bear; and, to make a diversion in their favor, it was necessary to press the flank attack with all possible vigor, and thus the angle where Ayres joined the right of our cavalry now became the key to the enemy's position. If this could be gained, Ayres's infantry would completely enfilade their line on the White Oak Road and render the direct assault comparatively easy. But if the enemy could hold our infantry in check, they could most probably repulse the cavalry with heavy loss; for their works were strong and difficult to approach in front, and from them they could, while completely sheltered, pour out a deadly fire. It was vital, then, that the flank of the enemy's line should be promptly attacked and broken; and the burden of this necessity now devolved upon Ayres's division, owing to the defection of Crawford's. Here General Sheridan remained, encouraging Ayres's officers and men by his fiery enthusiasm, his reckless disregard of danger, and his evident entire belief in victory. Already he had brought order out of confusion by his magnetic example, and had turned about the panic-stricken regiments and brought their faces to the foe again. Now, when the line was steadied and was moving forward to the attack, he took his colors in his hand, and where the fire was hottest led the men on, "Rienzi" plunging wildly under him, mad with the excitement of the roaring musketry, the hissing of the leaden shower, and the crashing of the troops through the woods. Here a ball went through the middle of the flag, and the sergeant who had been carrying it was killed; Captain McGonigle, our quartermaster (badly wounded at Cedar Creek), was hit again in the side, and two or three of the staff officers had their horses shot.

But it is not to be understood that General Ayres and all his officers did not do their duty; it was not because they failed in anything that General Sheridan remained with this division, but because this was the vital point, because here, where the enemy was weak, the victory must be inaugurated.

On the left of Ayres's division was the brigade of the young and brave General Winthrop, who rode into the woods as jauntily as if they held no danger, decidedly the best-dressed man on the field. Catching sight of him as he advanced, General Sheridan sent a staff officer to tell him that he would probably encounter the right of our cavalry, and warned him to be careful of firing upon them by mistake. Bullets were clipping through the branches about him, but Winthrop, who was calmly puffing a fresh cigar, smiled pleasantly, and said he understood the position of the cavalry and would keep a sharp look out for them; then, turning his horse, he called out, "Move in lively there, men! move in lively!" and was hardly lost among the trees before he was struck down mortally wounded. From right to left the whole division is now engaged; great shocks of musketry thundering back and forth through the dark woods; and now, moving forward, our men for the first time see the opposing force, strongly posted in a fortified line perpendicular to the White Oak Road; then there is a charge—a simultaneous rush—and our men are soon on the works sweeping all before them, and the left flank of the enemy is broken up past mending, Ayres's division capturing all who defended it.

Concerning this assault General Ayres says: "The troops were pushed forward, and soon came upon the left flank of the enemy, which was thrown back at right angles with his main line, and covered by a strong breast-work screened behind a dense undergrowth of pines, and about one hundred yards in length. This breast-work my troops charged, and took it at the bayonet's point, capturing, in carrying it, over one thousand prisoners and several battle-flags. Halting there a short time, by General Sheridan's orders, till it was apparent that the enemy were giving way generally, I pushed forward rapidly," etc. While Ayres is breathing his men, then, let us go back half an hour, and cross the White Oak Road with Crawford's division on his right.

When Ayres had crossed and found himself pretty warmly engaged, as we have seen, he at once began to change front to the left, and in doing so employed a tactical movement which put him in advance of Crawford and opened a gap between them. Crawford, finding Ayres's command fighting, should have gone to his support by a similar manœuvre, and closed up this gap; but he did not. He moved straight on, notwithstanding the orders of General Warren and General Sheridan to get his command quickly to the support of Ayres. General Warren says: "Orders were sent by me to General Crawford to oblique his division to the left and close up this interval." And most of our staff officers were repeatedly sent off on the same errand. Concerning this gap General Crawford reports: "The connection between the second division and my line could not be maintained. I received an order from both General Sheridan and General Warren to press rapidly forward," etc. And General Warren continues: "Orders were sent to General Griffin by several staff officers to move also obliquely to the left, and come in to the support of General Ayres. * * * * The time which elapsed before hearing from General Crawford or General Griffin convinced me that they must have passed on beyond the right of General Ayres. Leaving sufficient means to send any important information after me, I then rode rapidly to the right, and was received with a considerable fire from the enemy across the open field. As I afterward learned, this fire occasioned some unsteadiness in General Ayres's right, and also caused the left of General Crawford to oblique to the right, so as to keep the protection of the ridge and trees;" that is, while

Crawford's division was being ordered every moment to oblique to the left and rejoin Ayres, who was now heavily engaged, it was obliquing to the right, and so going far away from the battle. General Warren goes on to say: "I remained till General Griffin arrived with his division, when I directed him to attack the enemy on the right of General Ayres, and this he proceeded to do."

Crawford is given up for the time, and Griffin comes to the front; and as we have followed General Ayres into the enemy's works, let us now move with Griffin from the point where General Warren says he met him. General Griffin reports, speaking of the same point: "Finding nothing in front save cavalry videttes, and there being heavy volleys of musketry to the left and rear, the division was halted, and, upon a personal examination, it was found that the enemy was moving up the White Oak Road. Immediately the division was faced by the left flank and marched some four or five hundred yards, when its direction as to the line of battle was changed perpendicularly to the left, and moved down at a double quick upon the enemy, who was visible some three-quarters of a mile distant moving up the White Oak Road. The enemy's rifle-pits were taken, together with about fifteen hundred prisoners. Here a little confusion resulted from the troops exchanging shots with the cavalry, who were coming up in front of the enemy's works." It will be perceived that General Griffin did what General Crawford ought to have done. Not satisfied with the slow process of obliquing, he *faced* his command to the left, and marched directly across Crawford's wake toward the White Oak Road until he came within striking distance, and then formed line and charged rapidly down upon the now retreating enemy; for the force that he saw moving up the White Oak Road was falling back before Ayres's division, which by this time was again advancing, and, together with the cavalry, driving the enemy toward Five Forks.

Before returning to General Warren, the attention of the reader is asked to the fact that General Griffin does not mention meeting him, nor does he say anything of his instrumentality in accomplishing these results, but, on the contrary, says he was led to make these movements "upon a personal examination." Had General Griffin felt that the credit of his movement was due to General Warren it is strange he did not so report, since General Warren says: "I have seen nearly all the principal officers of my command, and all unite in telling me that they regard my treatment as unjust. General Griffin assured me he would so express himself at suitable opportunity to General Sheridan." In regard to the battle General Warren continues: "I then rode back to General Ayres's position, and found that he had captured the enemy's extreme right and some thousand prisoners. This information I sent to General Griffin, and then rode as rapidly as possible to direct General Crawford as circumstances might require." Moving from left to right we come now to Crawford, who has encountered the enemy beaten and retreating from Five Forks by the Ford Road, and trying to get across Hatcher's Run. This was where MacKenzie was ordered to go with his cavalry, but Crawford's division had crowded him over to the other side of the Run. MacKenzie says: "General Sheridan in person gave me orders to draw in the advance of my command in the direction of the Forks, and move round on the right of the infantry. The movement contemplated was thoroughly understood by me, but I found that the infantry extended so far to the right as to place me on Hatcher's Run, which I crossed and almost immediately recrossed, as there appeared to be no force in my front, and as the fighting seemed to be going on fiercely at the Forks, I judged my presence there was required." When, after recrossing the Run, MacKenzie reached the Ford Road, General Crawford had already crossed it, and was engaged with the enemy, and reports as follows: "Just at this point the enemy opened on my center and left a very heavy fire. * * * Major-General Warren arriving on the field at that moment, directed me to advance immediately down the Ford Road, and General Coulter's brigade was selected for that purpose." He goes on to say that "this force captured a battery of four guns and the battle-flag of the Thirty-Second Virginia Infantry. We then changed direction, and advanced again in a southwest direction, the enemy flying before us, though keeping up a desultory firing." The force which Crawford met here had turned its back upon the White Oak Road, and was probably trying to escape; one brigade was sufficient to disperse it, and as for the battery it was an easy prize, for we learn from General Warren that "three guns of the captured battery were found on the road, where they had been stopped in their attempt to escape northward;" while of Crawford's fight he says: "General Crawford's troops soon encountered a stiff line of the enemy formed to meet him, and from the fire of which General Coulter's brigade suffered severely. The contest, however, was short, for the enemy, now pressed front, flank, and rear, mostly threw down their arms." We shall now see who stopped the guns that General Crawford makes mention of.

After a short rest in the captured works (a halt being ordered there by General Sheridan to enable the other divisions to get in the rear of the enemy), General Ayres's division again advanced, together with the cavalry, which had also gained the angle of the enemy's works, and now connected with Ayres. Flanked by Ayres, and assailed in front by the cavalry along the White

Oak Road, the enemy fell back, fighting, toward Five Forks, and, as we have seen, had Griffin down upon them before they reached there. It will be remembered that some confusion was caused in Griffin's command by his troops exchanging shots with the cavalry. That Merritt's men should fire on his was a very natural mistake, for Griffin advanced from the rear of the enemy's works, while the cavalry charged them in front, and not seeing Griffin's movement on the other side, the force behind the works was taken to be rebels, as a matter of course, and therefore parties to be fired at; but the error was shortly discovered, and then the pursuit was renewed by Griffin—Ayres and the cavalry still pushing on. Let us now take up General Griffin's narrative where we dropped it in the enemy's works when he captured the prisoners. "After a few minutes' delay, the line of battle was again changed perpendicularly to the White Oak Road and the enemy's works. The command was then pushed forward along the rifle-pits, capturing prisoners and driving the enemy before it until they advanced to the Five Forks, where the cavalry and infantry met, capturing five guns and several caissons; and the third brigade, first division, taking on the Ford Road a train of wagons and ambulances belonging to Pickett's division. About this point Major-General Sheridan in person directed me to take command of the Fifth Corps and push the enemy down the White Oak

Road. I immediately directed General Ayres and the other commanders to push forward with all possible dispatch, and the pursuit was kept up until after dark, when the command was halted, the cavalry having pushed to the front, out of sight and hearing of the infantry." Great success had been achieved already; but when the infantry of Griffin and Ayres met the cavalry at Five Forks and charged the battery and captured it, a great *victory* was achieved, and nearly all that was left of the enemy fell into our hands; and these were the guns that were stopped on the road, trying to escape northward. After this, retreat was only a rout.

It has been seen, in Griffin's report, that at the Five Forks he was put in command of the Fifth Corps by General Sheridan in person; and it was at this time, therefore, that General Warren was relieved. Let us briefly recapitulate the history of the battle as given by General Warren and the reports we have quoted, before judgment is passed on General Sheridan's action. We know how, before the battle began, General Sheridan found fault with General Warren's indifference and want of confidence. In Ayres's first attack the door of the enemy's position was broken in; and while some of the troops of his division faltered, and General Sheridan rallied them, General Warren was occupied elsewhere. He says: "While giving orders thus, I did not think it proper to leave my place in the open field; because it was one where my staff officers, sent to different parts of the command, could immediately find me on their return. * * * It may be that at this time it was that General Sheridan thought I did not exert myself to inspire confidence in the troops that broke under a not very heavy fire. There was no necessity for my personal presence for such purpose reported from any part of the field." When this division was led to the assault of the enemy's line, and General Sheridan, with his flag in his hand, cheered on the foremost, General Warren was at "the Chimneys" with General Griffin, for he says, "I then rode back to General Ayres's position, and found that he had captured the enemy's extreme right and some thousand prisoners." General Griffin does not acknowledge to have been instructed by General Warren in regard to his successful movements; and it is therefore to be presumed that General Sheridan did not recognize his influence from that part of the field. In the decisive assault at the Five Forks, we see by General Crawford's report that General Warren was on the Ford Road with him. At the Five Forks the day was decided and victory was assured; and yet standing where the victory was won and looking back upon the successive blows which achieved it, General Sheridan could nowhere recall the presence of General Warren, and could not feel the effects of his presence from any direction. If General Warren, then, was instrumental in bringing about the victory, General Sheridan did not know it. There has been no effort to distort the records that are quoted, nor to draw false inferences from them; and from these the reader can form his own opinion as to the propriety of General Sheridan's action—in whose behalf it seems just that the circumstances which actuated him should be properly explained. This is the sole object in referring to General Warren's publication; and but for it no reference would have been made to his removal from command beyond what is contained in General Sheridan's official report. It would certainly have been more satisfactory to all parties concerned, if the investigation which General Warren asked of General Grant had been permitted; but that it was refused is not at all the fault of General Sheridan. For reasons of his own, General Grant, before the battle of Five Forks, sent "unsolicited authority" to General Sheridan to relieve General Warren from command of the Fifth Corps, as General Sheridan officially reports; but he did not act upon it until circumstances under his own observation seemed to demand such action. Again, for reasons of his own, General Grant afterward assigned General Warren to other commands; but it is not possible, as has been inferred, that he did so through any intention to reflect upon General Sheridan's course, which he had himself suggested and afterward confirmed by declining to grant to General Warren a court of inquiry. Evidently, then, General Sheridan's action was satisfactory to the lieutenant-general, who, in authorizing the removal and in refusing General Warren's demand for an investigation, has assumed all responsibility in the matter; and if any reader is not satisfied with the evidence which we have adduced, and does not acquit General Sheridan of intentional unfairness or injustice toward General Warren, it is hoped that he will apply to General Grant for an explanation of *his* unusual proceedings. General Sheridan, not doubting General Warren's entire loyalty, nor his gallantry, which was above suspicion, sincerely believed that he was not in a proper frame of mind to conduct vigorous operations; that he overestimated the ability and strength of the enemy; that he hesitated to strike boldly, and impaired the efficiency of his corps by his own apathy; that in fine he was a millstone hanging about the necks of 15,000 men, and a clog to their steps toward victory.

But it may be said that selfishness and jealousy might have been at the bottom of General Sheridan's dissatisfaction. It is hard to see in what they crossed each other, or for what reasons General Sheridan should seek a pretext to dishonor General Warren. One had already far outstripped the other in the race: General Sheridan was a major-general of the regular army; and no credit he could win would bring him greater advancement, nor any that he might deprive General Warren of. Personally they were almost strangers, in their official relations they did not clash; they were not rivals, competing for rank and distinction, and General Warren was no more to General Sheridan than was any other general in the galaxy of stars which would disappear at the end of the war; search as we may for an unworthy motive we will find none, and we may therefore safely assume that General Sheridan was actuated by a simple and honorable desire to further the interests of the service. Believing in success himself, he would not consent to be hampered by an unbelieving and unwilling associate in command.

But "something too much of this." The reader will doubtless gladly dismiss the matter and return to the White Oak Road, and see what progress has been made during this digression, and learn something more of the faring there. The cavalry now have it all to themselves, and are galloping hot-foot out the White Oak Road as fast as they can get up their horses, which have been calmly awaiting in the rear the issue of all this fighting; for, except Stagg's brigade of Devin's division on the extreme right, and Colonel Coppinger, of Custer's division, with two regiments on the extreme left, Merritt's whole command has been fighting dismounted—Devin has been contesting with Custer for the honor of first foothold on the enemy's works, and both divisions

A FIGHT ABOUT FIVE FORKS.

have gallantly planted their colors there. As has been already told, the cavalry on the right gained the angle where Ayres assaulted, and then crept up with his infantry toward Five Forks as a fire creeps along the prairie. Farther on the troopers had joined hands with Griffin in the enemy's line; and now on the left, as the tide of battle set that way, a good many men were mounted, and when the battery was charged at the Forks, a number of horsemen joined in the attack. On so long a line it is impossible to say who among the cavalry won the most glory or who most deserved it; but at this central point where the guns were taken and the finishing touches put to a good day's work, the gallant Colonel Fitzhugh, commanding a brigade of Devin's division, rode his horse into the enemy's works; and if some brave fellows went with him, there were none who went before him. Here while the guns were belching forth the vicious canister, our men swarmed in like bees. The Confederate General Pickett, whose celebrated division held the Forks, told, at Appomattox Court House, how he was standing in the battery trying his best to check the resistless onset in front and flank, when a Yankee cavalryman, bestride a mule, jumped over the works and ordered him to surrender and be damned to him; and how he was almost surrounded before he could gallop away. With him rushed off the remnants of the enemy: some by the Ford Road, to encounter Crawford and MacKenzie; and some by the White Oak Road, to fall victims to Custer, whose cavalry every moment broke over the line here and there and dashed on in pursuit, followed by Devin and the infantry, which pressed out a mile or more beyond the Forks, and only halted when it was quite dark, and the cavalry was four or five miles in front and could find no organized enemy.

The object of the battle had been to break up this isolated detachment of General Lee's army, and to drive westward, away from Petersburg, any portion of the force that escaped; and we have seen how fully this was accomplished. The enemy's force consisted of Pickett's and Johnson's divisions of Anderson's Corps, and some cavalry, of which we saw nothing after the fighting began. Of these two divisions, there were captured between five and six thousand officers and men, and their loss on the field was heavy; they lost their guns and wagons and ambulances, and those who escaped, having lost their morale, threw away their arms. It is true that we outnumbered the enemy, but he permitted himself to be outgeneraled to a greater degree; he had foiled us in the morning, and reckoned that we had then exhausted ourselves for the day, and so allowed a plan for his destruction to be matured almost within sound of his works, and exposed himself to an attack by a superior force in a position which, if selected by us, could not have been more admirably adapted to his ruin. General Sheridan, who was untrammeled by orders of any sort, caught eagerly at the opportunity thus offered, and planned and fought a battle with intelligence, energy, and gallantry; and won a victory which has no equal in the war for completeness and productiveness of great results. It opened the way for other successes, and it was the inauguration of a policy which crushed the rebellion within ten days.

So soon as it was evident that the whole of Anderson's force was captured and dispersed, the cavalry was recalled, and General Griffin was instructed to countermarch the Fifth Corps on the White Oak Road, and go into position east of the Five Forks, facing Petersburg; for it was supposed that General Lee would make some effort to relieve Anderson as soon as he learned what was likely to befall him. As Griffin began to countermarch, the White Oak Road presented a scene of chaotic confusion and disorder only to be witnessed after a battle. Here and there huge camp-fires were already blazing; the most important duty of the soldier—defeating the enemy—having been handsomely performed, the next important duty—cooking coffee—had immediately succeeded, and the horses of hurrying staff officers kicked over coffee-pots, and had anathemas hurled after them as they galloped up and down; hundreds of soldiers called out for their regiments, and hundreds of officers advertised theirs for the benefit of those astray; for it was after dark now, and fighting so long in the woods had scattered the troops in all directions. Drums were tapped and bugles blown, and cries resounded for these *enfants-perdus*. The muddy road was blocked with horse and foot, and strewed with abandoned arms; and mingling with the crowd came wounded men, limping slowly back to hospital, or carried in blankets if badly hurt,—friends and foes alike finding help to the rear and treatment there; for enemies with bullets through them always seem to be reconstructed. Droves of silent "Johnnies," under guard, tramped through the mire, jostling against the noisy "Yanks," who were filling the air with yells and cat-calls—the effervescence of victory. Now and then a prisoner would seem to be glad for our success, or glad that he wasn't in for the next defeat. "What day of the month is it?" asked one of our men of one of them, who answered, "The first of April, and I'm happy to say that we've been April-fooled." He saw the beginning of the end; knew that the bubble Confederacy was pricked and on the point of bursting, and knowing how dreadfully hollow it was inside, he was not sorry to be provided with transportation to the North, there to look about for something to do when peace should come; for your willing prisoner don't expect to go home again if he can help it. In a little while order came out of this rabble on the

White Oak Road, and Griffin moved back to Gravelly Run Church, getting his corps into bivouac about 11 P.M.; and meanwhile Merritt's cavalry went into camp near the Five Forks, and MacKenzie remained on the Ford Road at the crossing of Hatcher's Run.

While these arrangements were being perfected, General Sheridan, tired out now that the excitement was over, lay stretched on the ground, with a saddle for a pillow and a roaring fire for a comforter, and sent orders and received reports, and gave points every now and then to the reporter of the *New York World*, who was sitting beside him rapidly writing that capital account of the battle, which afterward found its way into the *Illustrated News* of London, where it was highly commended as a model of war correspondence. General Griffin and General Ayres had wagons up already and tents pitched; but our headquarters were seldom very closely followed by the train—and never when fighting was going on. So when everything was in order for the night, we retired to the house of Mr. T. Bass near the church, to make a pretense of being sheltered for the night. It was the merest pretense though, as Mr. Bass's house was filled with wounded, and most of us were in the saddle till morning.

At midnight a staff officer was dispatched to General Grant, who still remained at Dabney's Mill, away off beyond the Boydton Plank Road

—probably fifteen miles from us by the road the rider must take to insure a safe conduct; and this way through the woods was shockingly bad, and filled with teams and wagons for the first two miles or more. On each side the ground was a bog, and the branches of the trees drooped low as those did which caught Absalom. Farther on, the mud grew muddier and the horse labored heavily; then came the loose planks of the Boydton Plank Road, jets of water playfully spirting from beneath; then the fording of Gravelly Run, more difficult to contemplate than to do, although this stream might be magnified through General Warren's report, as Cassius by his magniloquence magnified the troubled Tiber; then had to be gained the left rear of the Army of the Potomac without encountering the right front of the army of General Lee; but here was well met a courteous officer of the Second Corps, who informed General Sheridan's messenger that to pursue the course he was following would lead him into the enemy's lines in less than two minutes. This misadventure escaped, the messenger soon struck the worst piece of road in the world—a corduroyed lane leading through a chain of morasses from the Boydton Plank Road to Dabney's. Here Dabney could have run his saw-mill almost anywhere—there was plenty of water, and the corduroy was all afloat, drifting down to Dabney to be sawed. There were four miles of this, and then the rider emerging from the woods as "dark as winter," suddenly found himself in the illuminated camp of the lieutenant-general commanding. This was about 3 A.M.; but the staff officers were still sitting round the camp-fire, listening to the good news brought by Colonel Porter and Captain Hudson, who had seen something of our battle in the afternoon.

General Grant was abed, with one eye open, tucked into an army cot—an easy thing to get into, but a hard thing to get out of at daylight after a short sleep following a hard day's work. General Sheridan's message was verbal, and to this effect, that he had gained a victory, the results of which were recounted; that he had taken up a position fronting Petersburg, and was prepared to receive an attack from that direction, and that he proposed to march that way early in the morning, by the White Oak Road, and attack the enemy's right flank. Had General Grant any suggestions or orders? The lieutenant-general replied, verbally, that he had no orders except to confirm General Sheridan's intentions for the morning, which he should have himself suggested had he not felt confident that the general would, without orders, do what promised best when morning came; he was glad to know so early what General Sheridan proposed to do. He added that orders had been issued for a general attack upon Lee's lines at 2 o'clock A.M., but that the several commanding officers were not entirely ready to assault, and the attack had been postponed for two hours; meantime a heavy cannonade had been ordered until the assault should begin. He thought it possible that General Lee might desert his lines at Petersburg during the night and fall upon Sheridan to open a way for retreat, and therefore Miles's division of the Second Corps had already been sent to the Five Forks to reinforce us. He believed that was all he had to say to the general, who must be governed by circumstances in the morning, and use his own discretion. Back again then to the Five Forks; the Army of the Potomac marking its front now with quick flashes of artillery, twinkling like fire-flies, far away toward Petersburg. Horse and rider confess to be tired by the time they reach Mr. Bass's house, just at daylight, and find General Sheridan mounting and the troops filing up the White Oak Road; but staff officers and orderlies do that sort of thing every night in war times, and if there has been a victory, and there is good news to carry, it is jolly good fun. And just now, especially, nobody about General Sheridan cares for a night or two, more or less, in the saddle, for is not this campaign to be the last?

CHAPTER VI.

LEE BREAKS COVER.

GENERAL MILES had already reported his division to General Sheridan, and was now on the march in advance of the Fifth Corps with orders to attack the enemy at the junction of the White Oak and Claiborne Roads, where they were reported to be in heavy force. This, Miles did promptly and successfully; and before he was overtaken by Griffin, had driven the enemy northward across Hatcher's Run toward Southerland's Depot on the Southside Railroad, where they held a strong position and were prepared to dispute his further progress. General Sheridan, riding ahead of the Fifth Corps, caught up with Miles beyond the run, and found that gallant officer confident of being able to drive the enemy and very anxious to attack. General Sheridan authorized him to do so, and intended supporting him with Griffin's command; but just then General Humphreys—Miles's corps commander—came up with authority to resume command of his division, which General Sheridan at once turned over, and then, lest the enemy at Southerland's should slip away, rapidly countermarched the Fifth Corps to Five Forks, and crossing Hatcher's Run by the Ford Road, gained the Southside Railroad, at Ford Station, without opposition; thus placing his corps in flank and rear of the force confronting General Humphreys.

This station was reached about ten o'clock on this beautiful Sunday morning, not a shot being fired to check our advance to the celebrated railroad, for the possession of which so much hard fighting had been done in the winter, and for which General Lee had sacrificed Anderson's Corps the day before at Five Forks. But now he had no more detachments to spare; he had learned wisdom of experience, and though in the night he had sent a division to the station which had thrown up a strong line of works across the Ford Road, it was rapidly recalled and gathered under the wing of the main army, when he heard that Anderson's Corps was annihilated and scattered, and that this division was exposed to a similar fate. The earth was yet damp on their breast-works as we rode through, and some grinning darkeys hard by informed us that the rebels had "done took out" about two hours before. At the station, we found an abandoned locomotive and two or three freight cars, in which were loaded some medical supplies and a dozen of the enemy's wounded; and from the upper story of the station-house crept down some others sound in mind and limb, who had taken advantage of the fog of the morning to bid a long farewell to the trembling Confederacy. As their division moved away they had stolen into the woods; thence for greater safety to the station-house, "and so good-by allegiance." Evidently the ruin was beginning to crumble about the edges, although it was not yet known here that the main wall had been pierced and broken in front of Petersburg that morning by the Army of the Potomac, and that it was tottering and threatening to fall before the chief Confederates could stand from under. General Lee had had his hands so full that he had not even found time to give the alarm to Richmond, and while we were breaking the Sabbath in the saddle, the pious Mr. Davis was keeping it in church; and, just as he was listening to the prayer for him and his cause, a matter-of-fact messenger came in to say that both were past praying for and he had better cut his lucky. Mr. Davis's confidence was so far shaken by what he heard, that he questioned the safety of the Southside Railroad as a means of travel, and discreetly departed by the Danville Road, which the ruthless invader had not yet reached. We rather expected him our way when we heard the news from Petersburg; but he disappointed us.

The enemy's cavalry had collected in considerable force on the north side of Hatcher's Run west of Ford Station, and Merritt and MacKenzie, crossing the run to the west of the infantry, had gone to look after them; but they rapidly retreated before our troops, who now could be discerned moving northward across the open country to our left. Without waiting to hear from them, General Sheridan with the infantry moved on up the railroad toward Southerland's Depot, in hopes to catch the enemy there in flank and rear; but Miles, meanwhile, had been pressing them in front, and before we came within striking distance they took to flight in the direction of the Appomattox, vigorously followed by Miles, who captured their artillery and a whole field full of prisoners.

Just at dusk, some of our cavalry that came up with us and passed us *en route,* and Crawford, who led the infantry advance, overtook the rearguard of this retreating column and exchanged some good-night shots with it in the open country to the north of Southerland's Depot; but pursuit was useless after dark, and the command was put into camp. Meanwhile Merritt pursued the enemy's cavalry toward Scott's Corners, on the Namozine Road to the north and west of Southerland's, and rested in that neighborhood for the night, after an almost bloodless day of marching.

General Sheridan had felt a good deal disappointed in the morning, when he was obliged to relinquish Miles's division, for he thought there was a good opportunity to do a deal of damage to the enemy at Southerland's Depot; but now at sunset they had in the main escaped, and altogether this seemed a *dies non* with us, with our troops flushed with victory and in splendid spirits for a fight. Marching up the railroad, they greeted the general all along the column with such hearty cheers as had been seldom heard in the army since the old enthusiastic days, when everybody believed that the generals were born to command, and that every campaign was to end the rebellion. There was plenty of good news to sleep on, however, and there was no danger that the men's good spirits wouldn't keep over night, as they were not aware of the chance that the general thought had been missed, and were beginning now to lose their skepticism in regard to success, and to realize what a very fine thing it was to be a hero of the battle of Five Forks. What a theme for a letter!—what a card with a girl! As late as the middle of the night, some of the wakeful "boys," thinking over it all, startled the owls with sudden yells of satisfaction, and kicked the dying embers of their camp-fire into an astonished gasp of flame.

Early on the morning of Monday, the third, we were on the move again in a new direction and with a new object. Hitherto the efforts of General Sheridan had been directed toward breaking in upon the right flank of the enemy's fortified lines defending Petersburg; and that task was in itself comparatively a simple one, in the execution of which strategy was not necessarily involved. It is true that the fertile mind of the general had found occasion for a good deal at Dinwiddie and Five Forks, and had used it to good advantage; but a general, innocent of strategy, could in some way have attacked the enemy's right flank, and with superiority of force could doubtless have doubled it up somewhat, and perhaps have gained the Southside Railroad. But now was to begin another phase of war; the fortified lines were abandoned; the enemy had evacuated Richmond and Petersburg in the night, and were now in full retreat along the Appomattox, and without successful tactics could not be brought to blows. Wits were now to be called into play, and wits that must come quickly to the call; for we must hurry on in pursuit, and yet be careful in our haste, lest the broken fortunes of the Confederacy might be mended with a false move of ours. The questions to be determined were, what point General Lee would aim to reach, and how to prevent his reaching it. By these questions, suddenly proposed, General Sheridan does not seem to have been staggered at all; and his opinion, once formed, does not seem to have wavered for a moment. To the first question, he answered: Danville, North Carolina; and to the second, he replied: turn his flank; head him off; attack him—never mind the rear of his column; never mind the stragglers, but get to the head and front; stand across his path and cry "no thoroughfare," and let the enemy fight for the right of way. Having mentally solved this problem to his own satisfaction, the general proceeded to demonstrate it to the army, to the public, and to General Lee, as will now be related.

CHAPTER VII.

THE PURSUIT.

When Griffin broke camp this morning his men were marched off by the left flank, and soon had Petersburg over the right shoulder as they moved rapidly across to Scott's Corners, where Merritt was already with his cavalry. All along the road were evidences of the demoralization of the enemy, for it was by this road that their force had retreated from Southerland's the evening before. Flankers and scouting parties of cavalry were constantly bringing in scores of prisoners from the woods on either side,—prisoners who would throw down their arms at the sight of blue uniforms and respectfully request to be captured; a hundred were willing to surrender to one. They were lost from the main body of their army; they were hungry and tired; and if there was a Confederacy to sustain they could not find it in the woods, and gave it up also for lost. Three brass guns (light twelve-pounders) were lying deserted in a wood road near by, and their caissons kept them company in a field by the roadside, the mutilated wheels bearing testimony to a lingering love for their cause on the part of the drivers. Arms, ammunition, knapsacks, and some very seedy clothing dotted the line of march, and we had come up with Merritt before there was any indication of belligerent people in this direction.

He had found some cavalry to contest his march beyond Scott's Corners, and skirmishing now began to be heard in his front, but he soon brushed away this obstacle, and pushed on out the Namozine Road, meeting no serious opposition until he reached Deep Creek, where he encountered a strong body of the enemy's infantry, which he attacked with spirit and success, driving them from the ford, and pursuing them vigorously as they fell back toward the Danville Railroad to join the main army of General Lee. General Griffin followed Merritt all day but was not engaged; and in rear of our column marched General Crook, who had now closed up, the retreat of the enemy relieving him from guard on the south side of Hatcher's Run, where we left him on the day of "Five Forks."

As we rode along it was evident that the inhabitants now began to realize that General Lee had at last been overcome. From all sides they heard of his utter discomfiture; on every hand they saw the evidences of his defeat and rout; and they had given up the Confederacy, and showed signs of a desire to anticipate reconstruction. We found more Union men in Virginia on this day than all our travels had heretofore developed. Their own soldiers had proclaimed that the rebellion was "gone up," as they had flocked by in retreat, and the steadfast women who begged them to turn back and face us again, had been laughed to scorn, and told that fighting was "played out." The darkeys were jubilant, grinning vast grimaces of delight, and dancing fantastic jubas as we passed by. "Where are the rebs?" said the general to a gray-haired old contraband, who was leaning over a fence, doing uncouth homage, and flourishing wonderful salāms with a tattered hat. "Siftin' south, sah, siftin' south," said the old man aptly, for certainly in this fret-work of retreat the Southern army was sorely sifted, and the part which remained to General Lee was not much greater than that which came through to us.

The line of our march was parallel to General Lee's, along the Appomattox River—his army moving on both banks from Petersburg and Richmond, evidently pushing for Amelia Court House, on the Danville Railroad, south of the Appomattox. It seems probable that he selected this as the most central point for the rapid concentration of his army and the most available depot of supplies, for that he did not anticipate so vigorous a pursuit, least of all a systematic effort to bring him to battle for his line of retreat and supply, is evident from his subsequent movements and the events of the following day.

At night we camped along Deep Creek; and while the command was asleep the restless Major Young, with a few of his scouts, took a ride with the enemy's cavalry, which was moving off toward Amelia Court House, and kindly assisted General Barringer, who commanded the rebel brigade, in finding a comfortable campground. Young managed to lead him off a little from his troops, and then persuaded him, with pistols, to surrender, and brought him and a staff officer safely to our headquarters.

At daylight on April 4th our command was again on the road, separating now into three columns, for the covering of a wider territory— Merritt and MacKenzie striking off to the right, toward the Appomattox, following the enemy who had retreated before them the night before from the ford at Deep Creek; Crook making for the Danville Railroad, at a point between Jetersville and Burke's Station, some ten miles south of Amelia Court House, thence to advance toward Jetersville along the railroad; and the Fifth Corps, under Griffin, moving out for Jetersville, a station five miles from Amelia Court House, in the direction of Burkesville Junction. Merritt, as usual, flushed the enemy, and at Tabernacle Church had a severe fight with their cavalry and infantry, through whom he found it quite impossible to force a passage, although he made a gallant effort, for they were obliged to stop him there if they would march in peace on the south side of the Appomattox, he being already uncomfortably near their trains, from which he had snatched a goodly number of wagons before they could hurry troops to guard them. MacKenzie kept off to the right of Merritt, with whose day's work his own was almost identical. The Fifth Corps marched rapidly all day, and the head of the column reached Jetersville about 5 P.M., a march of some sixteen miles, but "long drawn out" by the very bad condition of the roads,—their normal and constant condition though; and if anywhere it is neglected to state that the roads were bad, the reader will please supply the omission, and not lose sight of a fact which adds much to the credit of all the troops, retreating and pursuing, for it is one thing to march an army over a turnpike and another to drag it through Virginia mud.

Before reaching Jetersville two or three of our staff, with a small mounted escort, went off to the left to get on to the Danville Railroad and learn the news, if there was any. At Scott's Mill, on West Creek, they were filling their empty grain bags, when a scout of Young's, passing that way, rode up to say that the rebel army was at Amelia Court House and was advancing down the railroad. He was a little premature in his report—"went off at half-cock," as he himself confessed; but he proved to be correct in regard to Lee's position. This information was immediately sent over to General

Sheridan, who was moving with the Fifth Corps, and then the party quit the mill and the sable miller, who very much regretted that any of Mr. Scott's corn should be left behind, and trotted on toward the railroad. Squads of soldiers in gray, some with guns and some without, were wearily straggling on to Danville, and here and there could be seen a mounted man in gray, armed and equipped, listlessly joining them from a wood-path, slouching in his saddle like a tired trooper, and apparently with no object in life but to have company in shirking the calamities hanging over General Lee and those who remained with him. As the staff party neared the railroad these mounted men became evidently uneasy, and made furtive signs to prevent its closer approach; but they made no hostile demonstration, and seemed to urge the footmen to move on, as if they were satisfied that the strangers were friends. Then one or two of the gray riders cautiously advanced across the fields, and a couple of men in blue went out to meet them. When they came within earshot, the gray dragoons said: "Keep back out of sight; we are Major Young's men. The major's down the road a piece, and has a whole corral of Johnnies;" at which the blue men laughed, and riding off to the left, into the woods, soon caught sight of Young in a little thicket by the side of the railroad, his horses tied to the trees, and a score of his men with cocked carbines imposing silence on a regiment of prisoners, and bagging the unsuspecting game which his mounted decoys were leading in. Young chuckled and told the news, and expressed an eager desire for two or three hundred cavalry with which to surprise a lot of rebel horsemen that he knew of down the road, but lacking these, was amusing himself as best he might.

Stragglers to the front indicate the line of a retreat as surely as stragglers in rear guide the follower of an advance; neither are of any use to an army, and might just as well not belong to it for all the good they do, but they cling to its utmost limits, keeping it in view, and intending to rejoin when prudence permits. This light drift-wood in advance of Lee pointed out the course his wreck was driving, and, hearing of it, General Sheridan urged forward Griffin's infantry toward Jetersville, and sent word to Crook, down the railroad, to hurry on and join him.

At Jetersville, our advance captured in the telegraph office a dispatch just written by General Lee's chief commissary, ordering 200,000 rations to be sent up immediately by railroad from Danville to feed his army. It had not yet gone over the wires, and General Sheridan gave it to a scout to take to Burkesville and have it telegraphed from there, in hopes that the innocent commissary of the C. S. A. at Danville might be deluded into sending the supplies into our lines. The scout, by a plausible story, succeeded in getting off the message from Burkesville; but it is not known if the rations were forwarded. Probably they were not, if bad news flies fast as telegrams, for the wires could have flashed a plenty of the very worst to Danville that afternoon; but the finding of this dispatch proves beyond question that General Lee had no expectation of meeting any opposition in his intended march. He doubtless supposed that the pursuit would follow him, and he hoped to check it easily by bold stands of strong rear-guards and such obstacles as chance would throw in its way; and so his plans must have been sadly disarranged when some strolling cavalry he had at Jetersville sent word to him that the Yankees were pouring in there on horseback and on foot.

Either by his instructions, or from curiosity, or from an evident necessity to test the strength of these marplots at Jetersville, the Confederate cavalry promptly moved down to investigate; and, just as General Sheridan was sending an urgent message back to General Meade, there was some sharp and sudden firing in front. "Tell General Crook to drive them away," said the general, simply, and went on with his message. At this stage of the war, it was not considered necessary for our cavalry to make very elaborate preparations to meet the enemy's horse; we outnumbered them, and "had the morale on them," as the men used to say, and the general would grow very impatient and indignant if there was much firing at the front and no infantry opposing us. Now, before the officer got away to General Meade, Crook had cleared Jetersville, and held, occupied, and possessed the town, such as it was; and the leading division of the Fifth Corps was rapidly moving into line on both sides of the railroad fronting Amelia Court House.

Here was Lee's opportunity for escape, if he was in a condition to avail himself of it. Confronting his Army of Northern Virginia was one division of cavalry, and the head of one corps of infantry, boldly placed across his path in battle array, with no force within supporting distance; Merritt and MacKenzie were fighting Lee's flankers miles away on our right; the Army of the Potomac was at Deep Creek—a long day's march to Jetersville; and the Army of the James, moving down the Southside Railroad, was not yet near enough to Burkesville Junction to intercept the enemy there if he should cut his way through our force at Jetersville. All these thunderbolts launched at Lee would waste themselves in mid-air, if he could reach Burkesville first; for a stern chase is a long one, and our only hope of destroying or capturing his army lay in our ability to bring him to battle for his line of march. We have said already that General Sheridan fully appreciated this fact, and it is owing to his lively recognition of it that we now see him putting his small isolated force into position, throwing up breast-works as they come into line, and sending word to General Meade to hurry on and reinforce him, lest Lee should escape.

The galloping messenger is soon out of sight of Jetersville, making the best of his way against the adverse current of the Fifth Corps, through whose ranks he is at first obliged to tack like a schooner working up against wind and tide; but after a mile or two he has left them behind, except the stragglers, who lag along after the column, and drag their feet as if they were lost in thought determining some most important matter, and doubtless will soon halt between two opinions and lie down for the night. It is a good long ride to Deep Creek, whose banks we had left at early dawn, before the larks sang "hymns at heaven's gate," and it is well into the night before General Sheridan's officer gains the headquarters of General Meade and tells his errand to General Webb, the chief of staff—for after reaching the camp of General Meade's troops, it is no easy matter to learn his whereabouts in the dark; the staff officers having quitted the roads and gone to sleep, and the men standing about the fires not knowing and not caring for anything under the stars so much as for their supper, which is stewing on the crackling rails. General Meade had established himself for the night in a large house beyond Deep Creek, and the tents of his staff were pitched outside; and behind the house General Humphreys, commander of the Second Corps, with his staff, was partaking of a dinner fit "to set before a king," to which in good time the hospitable general ushered in General Sheridan's hungry courier, who here records his hearty thanks. General Meade was quite unwell, and had taken to his cot, but the chief of staff immediately delivered to him General Sheridan's message, and he then called for the messenger and asked him to repeat what General Sheridan had said—which was to this effect: that he was at Jetersville with the Fifth Corps throwing up some earth-works, and in hopes to be able to hold that point; that Lee without doubt was at Amelia Court House, but five miles distant, and would in all probability endeavor to break through to Burkesville; that this seemed to him a crisis in Lee's affairs and ours; that in his opinion if Lee could be balked here his army would be "bagged;" and to win this result he urged upon General Meade the great importance of forsaking everything, but arms and ammunition, and at any sacrifice hurrying on to the Danville Railroad.

The commander of the Army of the Potomac responded cheerily to this summons. He said: "Do I understand you to say that in General Sheridan's opinion Lee's army will be destroyed or captured if my troops gain the Danville Railroad to-morrow morning?" and being answered yes, he went on to say that his men had undergone great privations in marching, in want of food, and in the severe labor of helping the trains through the mud; all day long they had been corduroying roads, and had only just gone into camp; the supply wagons were still far in the rear and the men had no rations in their haversacks. "Still," he said, "everything must be given up for the good of the cause;" and he immediately issued an order of march for 2 o'clock A.M., stating that the distinguished General Sheridan had notified him from the front that the capture of Lee was now possible, and calling on the troops to submit to fatigue and hunger with the same alacrity and courage they always displayed upon the battle-field. Staying their appetites with this, "the weary boys" (as General Milroy called them, after his unlucky fight at Winchester), turned out from beneath their shelters, with their teeth chattering in the chill air, and set out for Jetersville, starvation, and glory. Like enough they didn't entirely believe in "the distinguished General Sheridan," and wished he had gone to bed and kept quiet, instead of sending back his dashed assurances to get them up in the middle of the night—"bad luck to this marching." But they trotted on cheerfully, with light hearts and light haversacks, that the general might not say it was their fault if Lee should escape. Before General Meade broke up his camp, other staff officers from Jetersville came in hurriedly with messages from General Sheridan, and rode by with dispatches for General Grant, all of one import—all urging haste at any cost.

Meanwhile Merritt had been recalled from Tabernacle Church and was on his way to Jetersville when the head of General Meade's command encountered his cavalry about 3 A.M. The double column crowded the road somewhat and delayed the infantry considerably until Merritt's troopers had all passed by, when the march was vigorously renewed; and the Second Corps, in advance, pressed on toward the railroad as fast as the night and the mud would permit. General Sheridan's messengers, reaching his headquarters before daylight, reported to him the progress of Merritt and General Meade, and then caught a cat-nap before the early breakfast to which the first rays of the sun would certainly ring the bell.

Everything was quiet in front of Jetersville all night, and the troops that had reached there had a good night's rest behind the earth-works they had hastily constructed, waking refreshed, and ready for the next stage on the road to the ruin of Lee. When the sun was well up, and the enemy still made no demonstration, it occurred to General Sheridan that Lee perhaps had decided to dodge the issue of a fight at Jetersville, and was trying to make his escape by passing around the obstacle which he fancied he could not overcome. General Crook was therefore ordered to send out General Davies's brigade of cavalry toward Fame's Cross Roads, five miles on our left, as we looked toward Amelia Court House; and this curling reconnoissance, thrown out like a lasso, soon discovered that the general's suspicions were founded in fact, for the wily foe was already trundling his wagons through the Cross Roads when General Davies came in sight and made for them with a view-halloo which startled the jolly wagoners, and brought out the Confederacy, mounted, to their defense. But it had not been often in the war that our cavalry had caught sight of the enemy's trains. Ours they had often defended, but theirs they had seldom attacked; and now the force which opposed them was blown away in the wind of their wild gallop as they dashed upon them and despoiled them; soon they were rifled of all their valuables, which were not many, and then the quaint vehicles were burned, and the C. S. A., branded on the dingy covers, was illuminated for a moment by the flames, and then curled slowly up into a flimsy tissue and disappeared in smoke. General Davies destroyed about one hundred and eighty wagons, and brought back to Jetersville a thousand prisoners, five pieces of artillery, some battle-flags, and several hundred mules—sorry looking, but no doubt glad to be captured, for the flying Confederacy had no time to feed, and no feed to give if there had been time, while under the beneficent flag of the Union even a mule could better himself and get fat again while the hair was growing to cover up the C. S. A. on his shoulder. It may be remarked, in passing, that one point of difference between this mule and his late master is that the latter won't consent to be fattened except upon his own terms, with the express stipulation that the C. S. A. shall not be covered up, but be blazoned as when he first was branded.

Sending his plunder in advance toward Jetersville, General Davies soon found himself hard pressed in rear and flank by a strong force of the enemy, who, learning of his raid, had moved rapidly out from Amelia Court House to intercept him; it was found necessary to hurry Gregg's and Smith's brigades, of Crook's division, to his support; and the sharp fighting that at once ensued seemed to indicate that Lee had at last determined to attempt an escape by the way of the Danville Railroad. Meanwhile Merritt's cavalry and the Second Corps had nearly all reached Jetersville, and General Sheridan no longer felt anxious as to the possibility of Lee's breaking through our line. General Meade had come up, too, and being the senior officer would naturally have assumed command of the infantry, but he was still feeling very unwell, and asked General Sheridan to put the Second Corps in position, while he retired to a little house where we had camped the night before.

Shortly after the arrival of General Davies's spoils a negro reached our headquarters, bearing a small note, which a Confederate officer had intrusted to his care to deliver to his mother. It was dated Amelia Court House, April 5th, and read thus: "Our army is ruined, I fear. We are all safe as yet. Theodore left us sick. John Taylor is well; saw him yesterday. We are in line of battle this ev'g. General Robert Lee is in the field near us. My trust is still in the justice of our cause. General Hill is killed. I saw Murray a few moments since; Bernard Perry, he said, was taken prisoner, but may get out. I send this by a negro I see passing up the railroad to Michlenburg. Love to all.

"Your devoted son,

"W. B. TAYLOR, *Colonel.*"

This intelligent negro was not going to Michlenburg, as his course indicated, but was on his way to join the "Yanks," but, as he explained, he didn't intimate this intention to anybody at Amelia Court House. Colonel Taylor seems a little ahead of time in saying "this ev'g," as General Sheridan had his letter before 3 P.M.; but the Southerners call anything evening that comes after noon, and no doubt it had seemed a long day to him, as he says "our army is ruined, I fear," and adds, "my trust is still in the justice of our cause," as if he had no longer much hope in General Robert Lee, nor in John Taylor, nor Murray, nor Bernard Perry, and the other plucky fellows who still stood by the sinking ship. This despondent letter from an officer high in rank confirmed General Sheridan's own impression in regard to the demoralization of Lee's army, and he immediately wrote the following dispatch to General Grant, who was moving upon the Southside Railroad with the troops from the Army of the James.

JETERSVILLE, *April* 5, 3 P.M.

To LIEUTENANT-GENERAL U. S. GRANT:

GENERAL—I send you the inclosed letter, which will give you an idea of the condition of the enemy and their whereabouts. I sent General Davies's brigade this morning around on my left flank. He captured at Fame's Cross Roads five pieces of artillery, about two hundred wagons, and eight or nine battle-flags, and a number of prisoners. The Second Army Corps is now coming up. I wish you were here yourself. I feel confident of capturing the Army of Northern Virginia if we exert ourselves. I see no escape for General Lee. I will send all my cavalry out on our left flank except MacKenzie, who is now on the right.

(Signed) P. H. SHERIDAN,
Major-General.

The lieutenant-general received this dispatch at dark, and set out for Jetersville without delay, instructing General Ord, of the Army of the James, to push on to Burkesville before halting for the night—thus placing a strong force in rear of General Sheridan and a second line in front of General Lee.

Meanwhile General Sheridan had put the Second Corps on the left of the Fifth, and Merritt went out to the left of the infantry; but he had hardly reached his position there and dismounted his men to await further developments, when the vigorous and sustained attack upon Crook's cavalry led General Sheridan to think that the enemy were perhaps about to try a general assault. The direction from which they approached suggested a change of plan on our part, and Merritt was quickly recalled to the right, and sent out in advance of the infantry on that flank. The ground about Jetersville is open, but Griffin, with the Fifth Corps, was intrenched in the edge of an oak wood, which concealed him from the enemy's view, and his line extended along a ridge which effectually commanded the wide valley that it overlooked; the ground occupied by the Second Corps was not so favorable for defense, and invited attack, as the land sloped upward from their front, and rather commanded it, and toward them the force of the enemy was tending. General Sheridan's impression was that if any attack were made it would, from the nature of the ground, fall principally upon the Second Corps, and then, no doubt, he intended, when they were well engaged, to dash suddenly upon the enemy's flank with Griffin and the cavalry of Merritt, which was now lost to sight in the valley beyond Griffin's ridge. This sort of flank movement is a favorite with General Sheridan, and had won him handsome victories at Winchester, Fisher's Hill, and Five Forks; but on this occasion, although everything on our side favored another trial, the enemy declined to be subjected to the experiment, and gave up their attack on Crook's cavalry before they came within range of our infantry fire.

Crook had his hands full though, and some fine fellows in his command lost life and limb at this late day. Brave young Colonel Janeway, of the First New Jersey Cavalry, bearing already thirteen scars, went down in a charge with a pistol bullet through his brain, losing to us a noble-hearted friend and soldier. Major Thomas, commanding the First Pennsylvania Cavalry, was badly wounded after having four horses shot under him. He had captured a gorgeous yellow sash in the raid on the wagon train, and had wound it about him by way of a lark, and, as some of us warned him, was taken to be a major-general at least, and became a special mark for the enemy's bullets. There were many more who fell, and every loss seemed heavier now because we felt that the fighting was nearly over.

The enthusiastic infantry, cheering everything and everybody from rabbits to generals, was obliged to go to sleep without a fight; and in the night Lee resumed his march by way of Fame's Cross Roads and Deatonsville, vainly imagining that it was possible to move with impunity upon a road which passed within five miles of Sheridan's cavalry, to say nothing of the eager infantry of Humphreys and Griffin.

Here Lee vacillated, faltered, and failed; for here he confessed his inability to make his way to Johnston by the road of his own selection, and there was now no hope that he would be permitted to join him unmolested by any road whatever. It was puerile to fancy that on a parallel road, only five miles away, he could march unharmed, with his flank exposed to our attacks and his retreating column liable to be cut into sections and destroyed piecemeal. But, unwilling yet to accept the situation and acknowledge defeat, he still chose to retreat by such avenues as offered—as a sulky chess-player, loth to succumb, will move his king from square to square, while his opponent pushes up the pieces which in a moment must inevitably checkmate him. With the hope of reaching Burkesville died the hope of saving his army, unless indeed Lee calculated upon our giving up the chase; and this he had no right to do, judging by recent events, for he could see well enough that we had dash on the prow and vigor at the helm of our craft, and that, instead of following in his wake, we were keeping to windward of him all the time, crippling him fore and aft, and watching for a chance to run him down. That he had such wild hopes of our giving up the chase, is the only defense that could be made to the charge that every life lost after this was sacrificed by him. As he understood his duty, it certainly demanded of him that he should try every possible means of escape before pronouncing all means hopeless, lest we should perhaps slacken pursuit and open a way for his safe retreat; but knowing that our policy was fatal to him, humanity demanded that he should give up the struggle, when once convinced that this policy would be persisted in to the end. The readers of history will judge for themselves how far General Lee is responsible for the lives which were given up to sustain and to break down his cause, after he turned aside from his chosen path at Jetersville and wandered off trusting to luck.

When we woke on the morning of the sixth, Lieutenant-General Grant was already at our headquarters with his staff, consulting with General Meade and our chief about the best mode of bagging the remnants of the Confederacy; for "bagging," which had its day once early in the war, was come into fashion again, and was believed in now with the old enthusiasm, and, be it said, on much better grounds. The Sixth Corps had come up in the night, thus concentrating the Army of the Potomac at this point. By request of General Meade, the Fifth Corps had been returned to his command, and MacKenzie had gone back to the Army of the James, so we had nothing but our own troopers now to depend upon for glory; but they could always be depended on, and that was a good thing.

The council of war was short; and, soon after "sun-up," we rode out in a heavy shower with Merritt's cavalry, following the trail of General Crook, who had already started for Deatonsville—a ville that is below Fame's Cross Roads, on the road that may lead to Danville and may not: we shall see. Before we caught up with Crook, the sun came out gloriously, breaking through the clouds to see how beautifully we managed these things in America after four years of war. It took the chill off and warmed "the boys" to their work, so that they cheered with delight, when in a gap in the woods, on the Deatonsville Road, were descried the dusky wagon covers of Lee's retreating train. But they were pleasanter to look at than to get hold of, as Crook discovered when he essayed to take possession, for Lee knew now what he had to expect, and prepared accordingly. Yesterday wagons were roaming about, half protected, in fancied security; but to-day they bristled with arms in the gallant convoy of Lee's forlorn hope.

> "In battle's wild commotion,
> The proud and mighty Mars
> Demands his tithes of hostile tribes,
> By death in warlike cars."

And so General Lee sent his wagons into the battle, and flanked their wheels with guns and muskets, — chariots with scythes having gone out of use somewhat in these modern times. Crook's men had no sooner shown themselves, than from round this warlike train there burst out an awful flame of fire and sulphurous smoke and curious heavy lead and iron balls, which none could see, but which struck down many a man and horse, and so we found that these eccentric vehicles were not to be had without a serious fight or successful strategy; and both being in General Sheridan's line, he was soon forming combinations for their capture by means of one or the other, or both.

Crook was ordered to make room for Merritt by moving off to his left parallel with the trains, and keep moving until he should see an opening for attack, and then to make it; Merritt, following him, would pass him then and attack farther on, while Crook should endeavor to get a foothold for himself, or failing in that, attract the attention of the enemy. It was expected that by the rapid execution of this manœuvre, one or the other would shortly gain the Deatonsville Road at some weak point and break up the enemy's march, and otherwise inconvenience him. As they moved off to test the merits of this idea, General Sheridan, retaining Stagg's brigade of Devin's division for any emergency that might suddenly arise, rode up a hill overlooking the

Deatonsville Road, and, planting his flag on the top, remained for half an hour peering through his glasses at the lay of the land.

The Army of the Potomac was now *en route;* and, moving west from Jetersville, the Second Corps, under Humphreys, had already engaged the rear-guard of that portion of the enemy's force which was moving on the Deatonsville Road. Across the country, a mile in front of General Sheridan's position on the hill-top, the rebel skirmishers could be plainly seen slowly retreating before Humphreys's men, halting now and then to fire, and finding this had no effect, doggedly moving back again; and we almost fancied that they shook their heads, as they shouldered their muskets, as if to say that it was no use fighting with fate any longer. They had three or four light guns, too, which spitefully cracked away every few minutes; but neither guns nor skirmishers did more than add dignity to their hurried retreat, which without them would have seemed a hopeless rout; and this slight semblance of organization and good order did not avail to keep them in our view very long, for by the time that Merritt and Crook were out of sight they also had disappeared in the woods, and the solid lines of the Second Corps had replaced them in the open ground in front of us.

Closely following the rear of Merritt's column, General Sheridan rode on then for a mile or more, until he reached a wide plateau overlooking the Deatonsville Road, on which the enemy's trains were rapidly moving, plainly in view, a thousand yards away, on high ground in the edge of a wood, an open valley intervening. Halting here, the general determined to make a diversion in favor of Merritt and Crook, who had gone farther on to look for a more favorable opening to reach the wagons, which evidently were strongly guarded at this point; for in the field below the road long lines of flanking troops were visible, with small parties of cavalry patroling their front to give warning of the approach of danger. It was obviously important to detain this large force here, by a pretense of attacking it, until Crook and Merritt could perform their errand, and the Sixth Corps, which was following us, could be brought up to attack it in earnest. So Colonel Stagg's brigade, which the general had retained for special service, was now advanced into the valley, with skirmishers deployed, and ordered to demonstrate as though intending to attack, while Miller's battery of horse artillery, unlimbering on the crest where General Sheridan was, opened fire on the trains on the Deatonsville Road.

All of our horse artillery was splendid, commanded by young and dashing fellows, whose delight was to fight with the cavalry in an open country, where they could run a section up to the skirmish line and second the carbines with their whistling shells; and if we were retreating and hotly pressed, as sometimes used to happen, the eager enemy was always held at bay by the rattling fire of these steady cannoneers, who would cling to a ridge till the gaining of it was hardly worth the cost. The cavalry had no better soldiers than the battery commanders and their lieutenants. Tidball, Randol, Fitzhugh, Pennington, Williston, Martin, Dennison, Eakin, Woodruff, Vincent, Calef, Butler, and the rest were out-and-outers — not very often heard of, and not much known beyond the army, but where the sharp fighting was they could be found; in the hardest marches they pulled through somehow; and in camp it was pleasant to see these swells, with their open jackets, tight trowsers with the double crimson stripe, their gorgeous badges, their riding whips, and their fast horses. Now, when Miller got his guns well to work, we were not surprised to see the trains stampeded; his first shot just clipping the fence by the roadside and glancing on through a party of horsemen galloping by at that moment. These we afterward learned to be General Ewell and staff, who told us that this shell grazed the cap of one of them, the wind of it nearly unhorsing him. Miller directed his fire at a little opening in the woods, and soon had the range so exactly that every shot was planted on the road, tossing the mud into the air, damaging wagons and demoralizing teams, and the unhappy teamsters, who, being darkeys pressed into the service, and not paid to be shot at, and having no sympathy with the cause nor care for the safety of the trains, objected to driving through Miller's Gap. Some of them took out into the timber, and some, who were arrested in the attempt, drove on only because to refuse was certain death, while Miller might miss them if they had good luck.

As we have said, the Sixth Corps was following us—the old Sixth Corps we used to call it, in memory of our Shenandoah campaign together; and the general had not long to wait before General Wright's staff officers came forward to report the progress of his march. Now the reader is asked to note the participation of General Wright and the Sixth Corps in the battle which soon will follow, because here again there is a question between General Sheridan and a fellow-officer, as whoever read in the newspapers the first official reports of the battle of the 6th of April, 1865, will doubtless remember. General Sheridan announces a victory won under his command by the cavalry and the Sixth Corps, and General Wright describes a similar victory won by the Sixth Corps with the co-operation of the cavalry. As these victories were one and the same, we now propose to weave into our narrative something of the relations of these two officers to each other, and of the part they played in the great engagement of the day, and in such a way as will not interrupt the natural course of the story. We have been going on so smoothly since Five Forks in our legitimate business of crushing the rebellion, that perhaps the narration has grown tame, and needs to be seasoned with the *sauce piquante* of a personal matter, and if so the reader will welcome the introduction of this element; but if any reader doesn't like the discussion of personal matters, and thinks them unworthy of the great events of the time, he is asked to remember that they have been always linked with great events, and to believe that in the moment of its greatest triumph our army was not a mutual admiration society. If all the adverse opinions entertained in regard to various commanders had been publicly avowed, the world would have wondered how such dolts of generals could have triumphed at all, and therefore it is not to be wondered at if occasionally in the history of the war we shall encounter a number of officers, each claiming or claimed to be the special hero of certain battles. For instance, Gettysburg. General Meade commanded in chief, and is popularly and rightly supposed to be entitled to the chief credit of that great fight; but there are those who say that he had nothing to do with it, good, bad, or indifferent. According to General Meade, General Sickels, by a false move, almost lost the day; and if we believe General Sickels, he didn't do anything of the kind, and his friends claim that *he* is the hero of the battle, while

General Meade was, by Sickels's audacity in engaging the enemy, forced to fight when he fully intended to retreat. It has been claimed for General Warren that he was the hero of the day, because of his excellent engineering in the selection of ground for the posting of infantry and guns; General Hancock and General Howard have each received the thanks of Congress for their valuable services on that occasion; General Doubleday has a grievance in regard to the battle; General Howe has an adverse opinion; and doubtless there is an impression on the minds of many distinguished officers engaged that Congress was blind to merit when it left them unhonored and unthanked. Wherever we look we will find bickerings and jealousies, no less in war than in society, until we find a cause whose grandeur shall swamp ambition and a society that will brook successful rivalry. So let us not be surprised if we find rival claimants for honors in our war, but study what testimony we can reach to learn whose claims demand our recognition.

But this digression is mostly by the way. What we have to do with suggests but does not fully illustrate it, for we do not mean to say that the matter at issue here caused any serious breach of personal or official relations; it is simply a matter of conflicting records, which we hope to adjust by a truthful account, leaving the reader to decide whether any conflict need have occurred, and whether strict justice did not for the moment desert a gallant officer who permitted himself to be swayed by an excusable *esprit de corps.*

While waiting for General Wright's column to arrive, General Sheridan took occasion to notify the lieutenant-general of the condition of affairs, and to urge again that the pursuit should be continued with unabated vigor. He seems to have feared that even the earnest commander-in-chief might fail to appreciate the golden opportunity which was now afforded for ending the matter. He wrote: "From present indications the retreat of the enemy is rapidly becoming a rout. We are shelling their trains and preparing to attack their infantry. Our troops are moving on their left flank, and I think we can break and disperse them. Everything should be hurried forward with the utmost speed." This dispatch had hardly been folded, and forwarded at a gallop, when the general had his field-book out again, scribbling away as follows: "The enemy's trains and army were moving all last night, and are very short of provisions, and very tired indeed. I think that now is the time to attack them with all your infantry. They are reported to have begged provisions of the people of the country all along the road as they passed." This was sent off galloping, too, and then the general seemed to think he had done all he could to feed the engine that the lieutenant-general was driving, and his nervous impatience increased to be driving one of his own.

Lieutenant-Colonel Franklin and Major Arthur McClellan, of General Wright's staff, had already come forward to learn the whereabouts of General Sheridan, and to report progress. Major McClellan had mistaken the track of some rebel artillery for our trail, and, riding confidently on through the wood, had run upon the flank of the enemy's force in front of us, and been unkindly greeted by a volley from those who caught sight of him; but, fortunately, he was missed in his quick retreat, and giving a wide berth then to the hostile wood, reached us safely as General Sheridan was ordering Colonel Stagg to make a more serious demonstration against the enemy's lines, to give color to the deception he was practicing with this small force of cavalry. Stagg's men moved out gallantly for a mounted charge, and, as seen from the knoll where General Sheridan was, there never was a prettier panorama of war in miniature than when this brave brigade trotted across the valley and began to go up the slope on which the enemy's infantry was now intrenched. A heavy fire met them, but they pressed on boldly, as if they had an army at their back, and the piff! paff! of their carbines echoed the sputtering fire from the enemy's hillside. As they neared the lines, they took the gallop and charged in handsome style, and some men and horses fell far up the hill, almost at the foot of the enemy's works. It was a most unequal fight, that could not last long without becoming a sacrifice, but, as a dashing diversion, it was a complete success, its boldness and audacity taking the place of numbers, and, supported by the moral force of Miller's guns, evidently seemed to the enemy a considerable demonstration not to be lightly regarded.

As the brigade fell back in scattered groups, to avoid the musketry fire, and re-formed in the valley to the left and front of Miller's battery, General Wright arrived upon the field, a little in advance of Seymour's division of his corps. He rode up to General Sheridan at once, and, after a friendly salutation, said: "Where shall I put in my men?" When General Sheridan was campaigning in the Shenandoah Valley, General Wright served under him, in command of the Sixth Corps, and did not now appear to feel that the old relations had changed at all, and nothing in his manner indicated any unwillingness to serve under General Sheridan again. Nothing could have been more prompt and soldierly than this first interrogatory as he glanced over to the enemy's slope and saw that there was work cut out for him there. General Sheridan officially reports (of which more anon): "I had been notified by the lieutenant-general that this corps would report to me;" and General Wright, finding his superior officer and former commander awaiting his arrival, reported to him accordingly;

and so to General Wright's very natural question the general as naturally replied, pointing to the valley below: "Put your men in here. We won't wait for the next division; I am anxious to attack at once." Here now was the head of the Sixth Corps going into line under General Sheridan's directions, and over the hills and far away was the cavalry of Merritt and Crook, "co-operating," by the general's orders, too; and if what followed was not owing to his plans, it must have been due to a dispensation of Providence, for without either the infantry or the cavalry the happy results we are about to record could not have been achieved, and none but the general knew what relation the Sixth Corps and the troopers bore to each other at this moment. It may be that the stars in their courses fought against Lee, but they were certainly abetted at this juncture by the ingenious devices of General Sheridan, who now, at the head of Seymour's division, moved down into the valley where Stagg was.

This infantry apparition seemed to disturb the enemy much, and before Seymour had begun to climb their hillside, they fidgeted out of their works in the open, and drew back to the edge of the woods on the road that Miller's guns had been shelling. The wagons had all passed now but a dozen or more, which lay scattered about in odd positions, badly knocked out of time by Miller's fire. This road we speak of leads from

Deatonsville to Prince Edward Court House, from where there is a pike, "a good broad highway leading down" to Danville (which place the enemy was "still a-harping on"), and it was about two miles and a half from Deatonsville to the upturned wagons in Miller's Gap. Along this road General Humphreys had been advancing with the Second Corps, following the rear of the enemy, whom we had been trying to annoy in flank. There is no road where Seymour was moving across the brown meadows, but just behind the enemy, as they stood confronting him, there is a by-way which runs off at right angles from the Deatonsville Road, and probably will carry the traveler to the Appomattox if he likes. For this intersection the enemy seemed disposed to fight, and Seymour's men, dashing gallantly up the hill, encountered a warmish fire from the inevitable woods, but they pressed on in unwavering line, and soon stood upon the road, despite the wicked musketry and guns, which retired then still farther for another effort.

At this point Colonel Sandy Forsyth, of our staff (whom shape of danger cannot dismay), penetrated the woods at the head of Stagg's cavalry, and discovered that the enemy's line had broken in two, that part was keeping the Court House road, while part was taking the by-way toward the Appomattox; and just as he returned to General Sheridan with this important information, Humphreys's infantry came out of the timber on the right of Seymour. Forsyth reported his discovery to both General Sheridan and General Humphreys, and the latter immediately deflected to the right in pursuit of the fragments which had broken off in the direction of the Appomattox, leaving to the Sixth Corps the remnant on the Court House road. Seymour then pushed on again, just catching breath in this short halt, and had hardly advanced a hundred yards before the shooting was renewed with increased vigor by the enemy, and with such good effect that after a few minutes' stubborn firing it was decided to hold on for Wheaton, who was rapidly closing up with his division, and soon ranged up alongside of Seymour, and was ready to try his hand. He undertook the left of the road, and Seymour was put on the right, Generals Sheridan and Wright, with staff officers and escorts, filling the gap between them. In this order the advance was quickly resumed toward Prince Edward Court House, while on the right of the line the bushes cracked under the tramping of Stagg's brigade of cavalry. Meanwhile General Humphreys pressed on gayly by the other road, and was soon engaged in an independent encounter there.

Finding our fire had so quickly doubled, the enemy now retired almost at double quick to look for better ground, and perhaps to overtake some part of their force that had gone before.

On through the jungle our men galloped in pursuit, for even infantry must take a gallop to get over the tangled undergrowth of Virginia woods. Almost a mile of this, hot skirmishing meanwhile, with yells defiant and cheers triumphant, and much music in the air from bullets, as if they played on the Jews-harp as they flew, and then we came in sight of land beyond the sea of trees—beautiful, too, as a wood-worn voyager could wish to look upon. Stretching far away to the right and left, until lost in counter-currents of table-land, is a broad plateau, shelving down gradually from the edge of the woods to Sailor's Creek (which trickles into the Appomattox): a shelf that will hold an army, but, until our arrival, upheld nothing save a barn and a tree or two, unless we take count of the weight of sacred soil; and beyond the creek is shelving ground again, woody there, and rolling, and

"An old road winding as old roads will."

The bulk of the enemy's force was across the creek before we caught a glimpse of it, but their skirmishers' bullets, game if they were rebellious, hummed the old tune still from this side of the water. The barn was about midway on our plateau, and, reining in "Rienzi" there, General Sheridan carefully studied the land beyond the stream through his glasses, while, under his directions, General Wright moved Seymour and

Wheaton down to the water's edge, the enemy's skirmishers falling back as they advanced. Immediately in front of where the general stood the ground is somewhat peculiar, and may be likened to the face of a man. Five hundred yards beyond the creek, and running parallel to it, there is a ridge crested with pine-trees, and this we will say is the top of the head, pine-trees at a distance answering very well for unkempt hair. Toward the creek the hillside is clear then for a little way, and just where we want eyebrows there are belts of timber spreading to right and left. Our face is native Virginian, so its eyes were shut that it should not see the impending calamity to the cause it then supported; but it has a Roman nose, which was very much at the service of the Confederacy. This protrudes boldly, and shows rather in profile from our stand-point, as it is turned down the stream, and was snuffing Humphreys's battle from afar. The lip is smooth, except some stubble of reeds that border the creek, which we will call the mouth; and Wright's men obscured the outline of the chin as they gathered about the ford and hurried over the water, which could not be crossed at every point, for, though the stream was not deep, its bed was very miry and quite impassable here except where our men were now. As they reached the other side, they rapidly deployed into line again in the face of a constant but not very heavy fire from the enemy, who had secured an excellent position on the farther side of the Roman nose, across the bridge and tip of which they directed their scattering musketry.

Meanwhile Merritt and Crook, with the troopers, had not been idle. While General Sheridan had been sitting in Miller's battery on the hill, and while the enemy was being driven from the Deatonsville Road and followed to Sailor's Creek by the leading divisions of General Wright's Corps, the cavalry had pushed on steadily in their overlapping movement to find a good place to get at the flank of the enemy's retreating column. They had found a ford a mile or two above us on the creek, then circled round toward the crest which represents the top of our topographical head, and were now looking about for an avenue promising entrance to the enemy's highway. That it should be somewhat debarred by hostile force and rude barricades on the perilous edge of the bristling woods, was to be expected and regarded as a matter of course, for they had not hoped to find an open doorway inviting such unwelcome visitors; so they felt their way carefully at first, testing the opposition warily lest they should become entrapped and lose the means of exit, as sometimes happens in war to those who enter hurriedly. A part of their force had crept up to the ridge in front of us, and, just as Wright's line was forming beyond Sailor's Creek, the heart of General Sheridan was cheered by a glimpse he caught through his glasses of a small party of our cavalry advancing directly toward the rear of the enemy whom he was about to attack. In another moment a huge column of smoke shot up into the air far away beyond the hill, and told plainly that somewhere thereabouts the bold dragoons might be safely placed, and that the enemy's wagon trains were furnishing the fuel for this "cloud by day." But conjecture became certainty in another moment, when across the creek came a galloping young cavalryman, who reported to the general that he had just been charging with Custer's division beyond the crest; had come through the enemy's line and couldn't get back, and seeing our troops advancing from this direction, had ridden down to us to escape capture and to tell of the doings of the cavalry. It was boldly done and well deserved reward; but in this country the generals commanding don't have the power to pronounce a soldier a captain on the spot, nor do they carry in their pockets the ribbons and crosses of the Legion of Honor; and so this young fellow, who was lost sight of in the excitements of the moment, probably rejoined his regiment that evening not at all aware that he had done anything remarkable. What he had to say now he said very coolly, and was listened to very attentively by the general, who asked him several questions and got very straightforward answers. From him, and from other sources afterward, we learned that the position of the cavalry at this time was on the left flank of the road which we were following; beyond the crest, of course, but edging up to it rapidly. Custer was on the right and nearest to it, Crook was in the center, and Devin was on the left—Merritt's divisions having become separated in the course of the overlapping movement, Custer not having yet broken off from the right to follow Devin when the point of attack was reached. In front of them they had found a swarming hive of the enemy, and though there was honey in it, no doubt, in the way of trains and guns, it was bitterly hard to get at. Crook had tried it first with as little success as in the morning, and was beginning to think that by going farther he should fare better, when Merritt came up to the rescue and sent in Devin and Custer on each side of him to make sudden grabs at the spoil while Crook should seem to be the only spoiler. This ruse was working successfully, and the enemy, in spite of his sting, was being hard pressed on every side. Crook had come pluckily up to the charge again and was riding at the breast-works desperately; Devin was pegging away and had gained the road, effectually cutting off retreat; and Custer was merrily sounding the advance toward the crest, and almost had his hands in the pine-tree curls that surmount it. Among them they had captured some wagons, which they had burned, some artillery, and prisoners to a large amount; they were still pressing forward ardently, and at any moment might be expected to crown the ridge and swoop down resistlessly in rear of the force that opposed our infantry.

By this time General Wright's troops were nearly ready to move on: Seymour's division had the right, and Wheaton's the left, and General Getty's was held in reserve at the barn on this side of the water, partly because it was thought the other divisions were strong enough to cope with the enemy's force, and partly because time was all-important, and some valuable moments would have flitted away in sending Getty over the creek. All the artillery of the two divisions in front was put in position on the high ground near the barn, and everything being now ready, General Sheridan ordered an attack—Seymour on the right to move straight on, and Wheaton on the left to bear to his right and gain the bridge of the Roman nose, and thus appear on the flank of the enemy who were opposed to Seymour on the farther slope. It was a hot ride then along the banks of Sailor's Creek, for though the enemy seemed in happy ignorance of the presence of our cavalry behind them, they evidently appreciated these designs in front, and before the orders were carried to begin the attack, the water in the creek was dancing over the dropping bullets which buried themselves in its bed, and, in the brave lines beyond, a good many men were falling. Seymour, on horseback, gallantly started his division in prompt obedience to the order, and in the face of a terrible fire led his men up the slope. Wheaton on the left had farther to go perhaps, and not being very warmly engaged, advanced more slowly (for at close quarters men move more rapidly than they do at long range), and so it happened that before he could gain the bridge of our nose and rest his muskets there to play into the enemy's flank, Seymour had passed the nose's tip on the other side, and, engaging nearly the whole of their force, was almost surrounded by a galling fire, which was cutting his troops up badly. Seeing their momentary advantage, this brave rear-guard of Ewell's essayed a counter attack, dashed down the slope at a run, and mingled with Seymour's men in the open; there was a moment of desperate fighting, almost hand to hand, but the left and center of Seymour's line, which were most exposed, were soon wrapped about in a deadly fire that human nature could not endure, and it bore them back and tossed them into the creek in spite of their struggles to repel its folds. Immediately in their front the rebels had a brigade of marines, who had been pressed into the ranks when Richmond was given up, and who, new to war and eager in the cause, now followed our retreating troops with an *élan* which was never surpassed; their standard-bearer led them on dauntlessly till he planted his flag-staff at the water's edge, where he defiantly waved the stars and bars, as reckless of his life as if the cause were worthy of it. But while the gallant sea-soldiers, seeking their element, were thus hurrying to the water, they were getting into much trouble on land, for, as soon as the plain was clear of our broken troops, eighteen guns of ours, which had been angrily watching from the plateau all this infantry fighting beyond the creek, opened their furious fire, and plowed the soft soil into rude furrows, that made graves for many of the enemy who fell before this awful mowing of shot and shell. Just then, too, the right of Seymour's line, which was held by the fine brigade of General Edwards and had not left the other side, came into action with determined front, and moving up along the stream aided the artillery with such a heavy flank fire that the enemy who had ventured to the water's edge hardly knew which way to turn. To stay where they were was impossible; to fall back to their old position was still to run the gauntlet of Edwards's brigade; on the other side of the nose they could see Wheaton moving up solidly; and so, in sheer despair, to get out of this dreadful *cul-de-sac*, many of them, with wild looks, floundered through the creek and gave themselves up as prisoners to the brigades of Seymour which they had just driven back.

General Getty's division now advanced to the creek to fill the gap in Seymour's line, and while General Wheaton gained the bridge of the nose and began poking the enemy in the ribs in a very hilarious way, General Edwards, by his steady fire, kept the ground clear on which Getty was about to form his line beyond the stream. A moment later, as the divided sections of the Sixth Corps swung together again like gates in this new formation, and just before they were closed, there was a mighty stir far up the hillside, and the irrepressible cavalry of Merritt and Crook, with Custer in advance, suddenly swept through the pine-trees like a gale.

It was all over now with Ewell and his men. There was one bewildering moment in which they fought on every hand; but then they saw how hopeless further fighting was, and threw down their arms and surrendered.

Here was the science of co-operation beautifully illustrated, and here was "bagging" indeed! Such a lot of game had never before in the war fallen victims to our wiles in the open field; and they were prime birds, some of them, in this covey under the pines. There was General Ewell, of hard-earned Confederate fame; Kershaw, as familiar to us as a household word; Custis Lee, who had been a bureau officer in Richmond, but drew his sword in front of the last ditch; Semmes, uncle or something to the bold buccaneer; and Corse, Defoe, Barton, and several others unknown to us. Besides all these, there were inferior officers by hundreds, and enlisted men by thousands—how many we never knew exactly, for there was no time to count them then, and afterward they were marched off to the rear by various provost guards of cavalry and infantry; and the question which ensued as to whether their capture was due to good management on the part of anybody, or to general good luck, or to a dispensation of Providence, included in its consequences a failure to obtain an accurate report of the results of this engagement. From the best information we could get though, there is no doubt that the day gave us from eight to ten thousand prisoners, and that Ewell's command was captured entire, with the artillery and wagons which had accompanied his column on the Prince Edward Court House Road. When the march was resumed after the junction of the cavalry with the Sixth Corps, there were a few stray shots to be sure here and there through the woods; but these came from scattered and insignificant groups which had escaped through the openings of the net-work which surrounded them, as grains of corn will drop through the coarse texture of a bag.

With Getty's division, as it moved forward for the attack which was about to be made when the cavalry *coup* put an end to the fighting, General Sheridan had advanced, and following the winding road which twists up to the crest beyond the creek, found that our topographical head had only a forelock of pines, behind which was a wide, bald crown; and on this open plain the general dismounted to rest, while Getty's divisions, by his orders, pushed on for a mile or two in support of Devin's cavalry, which had been sent to beat up the country still farther on, to see if perhaps there was any more game. It was long after dark now: we had almost used up the short April afternoon when the Sixth Corps first crossed Sailor's Creek; and the crackling campfire which was lighted at the general's headquarters served the triple purpose of a beacon, an overcoat, and a torch, as anxious officers hunted for him to get orders and give reports; as the roaring flame warmed the chill air; and as he wrote the following dispatch to the lieutenant-general:

CAVALRY HEADQUARTERS,
April 6th, 1865.
LIEUTENANT-GENERAL U. S. GRANT,
Commanding Armies of the United States:

GENERAL—I have the honor to report that the enemy made a stand at the intersection of the Burke's Station Road with the road upon which they were retreating. I attacked them with two divisions of the Sixth Corps and routed them handsomely, making a connection with the cavalry.

I am still pressing on with both cavalry and infantry. Up to the present time we have captured Generals Ewell, Kershaw, Barton, Corse, Defoe, and Custis Lee; several thousand prisoners, fourteen pieces of artillery and caissons, and a large number of wagons. If the thing is pressed, I think that Lee will surrender.

   (Signed) P. H. SHERIDAN,
           Major-General.

At the same time, by the light of another camp-fire whose smoke was blowing into our eyes, General Wright was reporting to General Meade concerning the operations of the gallant Sixth Corps. He wrote to General Webb, chief of staff, and first gave details of the fight on the Deatonsville Road by Seymour, and the advance toward Sailor's Creek when Wheaton came to the front. It is no use repeating it all here and going over that ground again, so we will only quote so much as alludes in any way to the cavalry—we cannot quote his allusions to General Sheridan from the fact that he forgot to mention him. He says: "In the first attack, a portion of the cavalry operated on our right flank; in the subsequent attacks, the mass of the cavalry operated on our left and the right flank of the enemy. The result has been a complete success. The combined forces captured five general officers, among them Generals Ewell and Custis Lee, and a large number of other prisoners."

This was a perfectly fair report so far as the cavalry and his own troops were concerned, and General Wright could not be condemned if he had expressed himself more strongly than he did in regard to the conduct of his own men; and it would be pardonable if he had claimed for them the lion's share of credit in this successful fight, for they had behaved all day with unsurpassed devotion, and had gallantly driven the enemy to a point where the co-operative movement of the cavalry could be utilized. If at the close of the game the cavalry seemed to play the winning card by throwing brilliantly upon the cloth their unexpected and resistless trump, yet looking calmly back to the burden and heat of it, nobody could deny that the partner had played good cards boldly and well, and deserved equal glory for the success and the heavy stakes that were pocketed. General Wright, too, might have claimed something for himself if his sense of propriety had permitted; for he bent his entire energies toward gaining this success, and seconded General Sheridan like a true man and a soldier. But that he did second him cannot be denied with truth. First in command, first to direct, and first to inspirit the execution, was General Sheridan; and as he now lent the prestige of his presence to these old followers of his in the brilliant campaign of the Shenandoah Valley, will anybody deny who heard them cheer him that it gave them a confidence which told upon the enemy? As he gave directions on every side as to how a division should guide its advance or how a brigade should be disposed; as he rode so far to the front with the skirmishers, that even General Wright suggested shelter under a knoll if only to save the horses; as he planned and directed the main attack against the crest beyond the creek, where he knew that the cavalry, following his orders, too, might appear at any moment,—did any one who saw him doubt that he controlled absolutely the movements of the Sixth Corps? It is no use to pause for an answer: nobody will deny. Therefore it may be claimed with propriety that it would have been civil, to say the least, if General Wright had casually mentioned General Sheridan, if only to say that he had been spending the afternoon with him.

But this so far is a mere question of proprieties; the more serious consideration of justice became mingled with it when, after Lee's surrender, General Sheridan, with a view to his own official report, requested of General Wright a report of the operations of the Sixth Corps, and General Wright declined to furnish it on the ground that he had already reported them to General Meade, to whose army he belonged. In this it is thought that General Wright, as has been already said, permitted himself to be swayed by his *esprit de corps*.

As the Army of the Potomac was justly proud of the old Sixth Corps, so it is very natural that the corps commander should be proud of the army and jealous of its renown; but it was hardly fair to steal the thunder of a deserving general to add to the volume of that which already belonged to the glorious A. P. General Grant seems to have taken this view of the matter when it was referred to him by General Sheridan on General Wright's refusal to send in a report; and as the official papers are brief, they may best tell their own story. Professor Coppée, in "Grant and his Campaigns," informs us that a paper bearing this indorsement was duly received at the headquarters of the lieutenant-general:

"Major-General P. H. Sheridan forwards copy of dispatch to General Wright, commanding Sixth Corps, asking him to report the action of that corps at the battle of Sailor's Creek, April 6th, and forward same; also General Wright's reply, who says he has reported to General Meade, under whose orders he is, and to whose army his corps belongs. Asks that General Wright be instructed to report to him (General Sheridan)."

Under which indorsement General Grant saw fit to write as follows:

HEADQUARTERS ARMY UNITED STATES,
Washington, May 8th, 1865.

Respectfully referred to Major-General Meade, commanding the Army of the Potomac, and attention invited to inclosed copy of dispatch, of date 6th inst., to Major-General Wright, commanding Sixth Army Corps; also to copy of dispatch to Major-General Sheridan, of date April 6th, 1865.

This corps was not by any order, at any time, detached from your command, but under my instructions to Major-General Sheridan, in answer to information I had just received from him, he was authorized to assume the command of this corps, when it joined him, and it is considered a matter of simple justice that its action, while under his command, be reported to him.

In your official report you will report the whole of the operations of that corps on the 6th of April, 1865, and General Wright will be required to make to you a report of the whole day's operations, including the battle of Sailor's Creek.

(Signed) U. S. GRANT,
Lieutenant-General.

The dispatch to General Wright reads as follows:

HEADQUARTERS ARMIES OF THE UNITED STATES,
Washington, May 6th, 1865.

MAJOR-GENERAL H. G. WRIGHT,
City Point, Va.

Please furnish an official report of your corps in the battle of Sailor's Creek, fought April 6th, 1865, to Major-General P. H. Sheridan. It was the intention of the lieutenant-general that (in the absence of other orders) when you joined Sheridan you should act under his orders, and he was so instructed.

A copy of this dispatch will be forwarded to Major-General Meade.

By command of Lieutenant-General Grant.

(Signed)   T. S. BOWERS,
Assistant Adjutant-General.

Thus the controversy arose and was settled in the army, but to people at home there was a strange inconsistency, which was not easily reconciled, owing to some further complications. In addition to the dispatch which General Wright sent to General Meade, General Humphreys, commanding the Second Corps, and who, it will be remembered, had followed the force of the enemy which broke off toward the Appomattox, from the Deatonsville Road, after Seymour's first attack, also reported concerning his operations and success. He had gone on swimmingly, capturing guns, flags, prisoners, and all sorts of plunder till the broken wagons and limbers on the road impeded his march. At dark he had been obliged to call a halt, being unable to get across Sailor's Creek, which crosses his road a couple of miles to the right of where General Sheridan fought. He wrote: "The wagons are across the approach to the bridge, and it will take some time to clear it. The enemy is in position on the heights beyond with artillery. The bridge is partially destroyed, and the approaches on either side are of soft bottom land," etc.

This dispatch, together with General Wright's, General Meade forwarded to General Grant, and said in their behalf: "I transmit dispatches from General Humphreys and General Wright, which, in justice to those distinguished officers and the gallant corps they command, I beg the War Department for immediate publication."

They were published accordingly, and so in the same issue of the newspapers was the dispatch of General Sheridan, and the following from the Secretary of War to General Dix, whose duty it was to deal the information which the War Department cut for him:

"General Sheridan attacked and routed Lee's army yesterday, capturing Major-Generals Ewell, Kershaw, Barton, Corse, and many other general officers, several thousand prisoners, and a large number of cannon, and expects to force Lee to surrender all that is left of his army. Details will be given as speedily as possible, but telegraph is working badly."

Certainly the enthusiastic Secretary of War made up to General Sheridan any deficiency of credit for that day's work. Where he got his information does not appear—perhaps a little bird told him—but all these dispatches are said to have been somewhat confusing to the eager and unmilitary readers of the morning papers, as apparently none of the numerous fights bore any relation to each other except in the overwhelming defeat of the enemy, who must have been badly used up indeed, they thought, if these several calamities had befallen him "all at once, and nothing first;" and they began to hope that so much disaster would cause the Confederacy to break up suddenly, "just as bubbles do when they burst." It is to clear up any remaining mist of misapprehension that may still befog the operations of this day that they are here so fully explained, and to demonstrate that there was but one battle of Sailor's Creek, which, from first to last, was fought by General Sheridan, ably aided by General Wright and the cavalry commanders. General Humphreys's fight, which was entirely independent, was no doubt a good one, and will some day be fully described, let us hope, but it had nothing to do with General Sheridan's operations, for the battle of Sailor's Creek was fought beyond the stream, two miles away from General Humphreys's troops, who did not get across that night.

When we struck off into these digressive paths, General Sheridan was sitting by his camp-fire in the plain on top of the crest where the fighting had ended, and now he is on the broad of his back, on a blanket, with his feet to the fire, in a condition of sleepy wakefulness which can only be attained through excessive fatigue and a sense of responsibility. Clustered about are blue uniforms and gray in equal numbers, and immediately around our camp-fire are most of the Confederate generals who have just been captured. General Ewell is the principal figure in the group, and attracts, though he seems to avoid, attention. He has plainly admitted that there is no hope now for General Lee, and has begged General Sheridan to send him a flag of truce and demand his surrender, in order to save any further sacrifice, but the general has made no further response to this than to urge General Grant to push on faster. Ewell is sitting on the ground hugging his knees, with his face bent down between his arms, and if anything could add force to his words, the utter despondency of his air would do it. The others are mostly staid, middle-aged men, tired to death nearly, and in no humor for a chat; and so the party is rather a quiet one, for our fellows are about done over, too, and half starved. To this sprawling party enter Sandy Forsyth, aide-de-camp, to announce that he has established headquarters in a lovely orchard, where tents are up and supper is cooking; so we follow the beaming colonel down the road for a mile and find ourselves quartered just in rear of Getty, who has gone into position for the night, Devin in front of him reporting no enemy.

We carried the Confederate generals with us and shared our suppers and blankets with them, as we would be done by, and after a sleep of hardly an hour, took breakfast in their company and then parted with it as we followed the general's swallow-tailed flag down the road.

This day, April 7th, we were left again with nobody but the troopers. The general had no orders of any kind, and we were as free as "birds that wanton in the air;" so we took a bird-line for what was supposed to be the enemy's flank and head-of-column, passing ahead of General Humphreys's troops (early birds, too), whom we encountered on the road he had followed yesterday—the enemy having retreated from his front in the night—and soon found ourselves in the open country, with nothing to obstruct our march but mud. It rained a little all day, just to keep the soil soft and make things pleasant and help the crops; but nobody ever noticed the weather or the roads now, since the earth and elements had combined at Dinwiddie Court House to mar our campaign. We all knew that was the worst they could do; and, measured by that standard, the present condition of things was in the highest degree delightful. If any one had complained, he would have been summarily told to go to—Dinwiddie. Our march took us over hill and dale, through all sorts of by-ways and wood-roads for the first ten miles or more, till we gained a decided thoroughfare leading to Prince Edward Court House; and meanwhile General Crook's division had left us *en route*, having been sent by General Sheridan on a reconnoissance to Farmville Station, where the Lynchburg Railroad meets the Appomattox River. We had suddenly transferred our attention from

furious gallop, while officers shouted "close up! —close up!" and tin-pans rattled, and sabers swung dangerously to and fro, blankets slipped, backs galled into shocking sores, feed-bags split open, and oats were sowed on the trampled highway; then there would be a shock as if two railroad trains had collided, and, pulled up with a sudden halt, the panting horses would gasp for breath, while the riders would wonder whatever had happened to the head of the column, to which nothing had happened at all. But we had changed all that now, and could march 10,000 cavalry on one road from daylight to dark, and never change the gait in a single regiment, and never turn a hair.

The general dismounted here, at the fence of a stiff old gentleman, who was sitting on his high piazza and scowling severely as we rode up. He was the typical Southerner of fifty years; his long gray hair fell over the collar of his coat behind his ears; he was arrayed in the swallow-tail of a by-gone mode, a buff linen vest, cut low, and nankeen pantaloons springing far over the foot that was neatly incased in morocco slippers; a bristling shirt-frill adorned his bosom, and from the embrasure of his wall-like collar he shot defiant glances at us as we clattered up the walk to his house. Prince Edward Court House was a stranger to war, and our indignant friend was looking now for the first time on the like of us, and certainly he didn't seem to like our look.

He bowed in a dignified way to the general, who bobbed at him carelessly and sat down on a step, drew out his inevitable map, lighted a fresh cigar, and asked our host if any of Lee's troops had been seen about here to-day. "Sir," he answered, "as I can truly say that none have been seen by me I will say so; but if I had seen any, I should feel it my duty to refuse to reply to your question. I cannot give you any information which might work to the disadvantage of General Lee." This neat little speech, clothed in unexceptionable diction, which no doubt had been awaiting us from the time we tied our horses at the gate, missed fire badly. It was very patriotic and all that; but the general was not in a humor to chop patriotism just then, so he only gave a soft whistle of surprise, and returned to the attack quite unscathed.

"How far is it to Buffalo River?"

"Sir, I don't know."

"The devil you don't! how long have you lived here?"

"All my life."

"Very well, sir, it's time you did know. Captain! put this gentleman in charge of a guard, and when we move, walk him down to Buffalo River and show it to him."

And so he was marched off, leaving us a savage glare at parting; and that evening tramped five miles away from home to look at a river which was as familiar to him as his own family. Doubt-

furious gallop, while officers shouted "close up! —close up!" and tin-pans rattled, and sabers swung dangerously to and fro, blankets slipped, backs galled into shocking sores, feed-bags split open, and oats were sowed on the trampled highway; then there would be a shock as if two railroad trains had collided, and, pulled up with a sudden halt, the panting horses would gasp for breath, while the riders would wonder whatever had happened to the head of the column, to which nothing had happened at all. But we had changed all that now, and could march 10,000 cavalry on one road from daylight to dark, and never change the gait in a single regiment, and never turn a hair.

The general dismounted here, at the fence of a stiff old gentleman, who was sitting on his high piazza and scowling severely as we rode up. He was the typical Southerner of fifty years; his long gray hair fell over the collar of his coat behind his ears; he was arrayed in the swallow-tail of a by-gone mode, a buff linen vest, cut low, and nankeen pantaloons springing far over the foot that was neatly incased in morocco slippers; a bristling shirt-frill adorned his bosom, and from the embrasure of his wall-like collar he shot defiant glances at us as we clattered up the walk to his house. Prince Edward Court House was a stranger to war, and our indignant friend was looking now for the first time on the like of us, and certainly he didn't seem to like our look.

He bowed in a dignified way to the general, who bobbed at him carelessly and sat down on a step, drew out his inevitable map, lighted a fresh cigar, and asked our host if any of Lee's troops had been seen about here to-day. "Sir," he answered, "as I can truly say that none have been seen by me I will say so; but if I had seen any, I should feel it my duty to refuse to reply to your question. I cannot give you any information which might work to the disadvantage of General Lee." This neat little speech, clothed in unexceptionable diction, which no doubt had been awaiting us from the time we tied our horses at the gate, missed fire badly. It was very patriotic and all that; but the general was not in a humor to chop patriotism just then, so he only gave a soft whistle of surprise, and returned to the attack quite unscathed.

"How far is it to Buffalo River?"

"Sir, I don't know."

"The devil you don't! how long have you lived here?"

"All my life."

"Very well, sir, it's time you did know. Captain! put this gentleman in charge of a guard, and when we move, walk him down to Buffalo River and show it to him."

And so he was marched off, leaving us a savage glare at parting; and that evening tramped five miles away from home to look at a river which was as familiar to him as his own family. Doubtless to this day he regales the neighbors with the story of this insult that was put upon him, and still brings up his children in the faith for whose dogmas he suffered. Doubtless, too, he considers General Sheridan a perfect gentleman.

After making some geographical inquiries of a smart colored boy, who seemed to know more than the white people hereabouts, the general borrowed MacKenzie again, and sent him off toward Prospect Station, on the Lynchburg Railroad, several miles to the west of Farmville, to learn if the enemy was moving that way; and to fill up all the chinks of time, forestalled other chances by sending a staff officer with a regiment toward Farmville, with orders to get into that town, if possible, and learn what he could of the enemy's doings. His party found no difficulty in accomplishing this, for Farmville was swarming with our troops when he came in sight. Crook was there with his cavalry, and was rapidly crossing the Appomattox River in pursuit of Lee's rear-guard; so was the Sixth Army Corps, and General Humphreys's Corps was already on the other side. Everybody, almost, seemed to be at Farmville or in the neighborhood, and no safer place to approach could have been found in the enemy's country. Everything was bustle and hurry; troops marched and countermarched in every side street, while the long avenue which pierces the center of the town was blocked with all the *impedimenta* of an army. Lee's artillery, from the northern bank, had been firing over the houses noisily, and the natives looked anxious and worried with the fear that a battle would be fought within range of their windows, from which they peered wistfully, flinching a little at every crack of the guns. In the middle of the town and the midst of the confusion appeared the lieutenant-general, serenely smoking on the piazza of the Farmville Hotel while farming out the remnant of the Confederacy to his various partners in the undertaking. He received the report of General Sheridan's whereabouts, and indorsed his intention of moving off toward Prospect Station to hunt for the enemy's flank and head-of-column. "Tell General Sheridan," he said, "that I think well of his movement in that direction. I will push on from here rapidly across the river, and send some infantry to follow him. I have written a note to General Lee, and I think perhaps he will surrender soon." This note was the first in the correspondence which is so familiar to all that it seems hardly worth while to refer to it, except that what has been written here already may aid the reader to appreciate the real condition of affairs when Lee replied to General Grant, who asked him to surrender because he thought it his duty to shift from himself the responsibility of any further effusion of blood, that he did not entertain the opinion General Grant expressed on the hopelessness of further resistance on the part of the

Army of Northern Virginia. What hope he had that he did not consider further resistance hopeless, does not appear in his communication, and certainly did not appear to any who followed him in pursuit, and doubtless to few who shared his fortunes. It is difficult to see what he expected to gain by further demur, or on what grounds he justified the losses that he must incur by still staggering on. It was time for him to drop his sword's point when honor was satisfied and there was nothing to gain, and only more life to lose by this reeling fighting his army was keeping up. They did it bravely, though, as if they saw beyond it all a promise of victory instead of defeat. Crook, pushing after them in too great haste, struck a snag on the hills beyond Farmville, where the enemy made a dashing attack upon his column, and before he could form line to repel them, whisked off with the head of it and General Irvine Gregg, who was riding at the front; and all that afternoon, until recalled to General Sheridan, Crook found them in such force and fighting mood that it was quite impossible to get among their trains, as he had amiably intended to do.

When the party which had left Prince Edward Court House as scouts returned as messengers from the lieutenant-general, they found the cavalry column already on the road to Prospect Station, and, after hard riding, General Sheridan was overtaken only on the bridge that spans the

Buffalo River. What he heard from Farmville strengthened his earlier impressions that the course he had chosen would lead him across the enemy's path very soon, so he went into camp after dark, near the railroad, in a cheerful frame of mind and with pleasant anticipations for the morrow. Meanwhile General Griffin, with the Fifth Corps, and General Ord, with a part of the Army of the James, came down to Prince Edward Court House from Farmville, and followed the trail of our cavalry; and Crook, by way of the railroad, arrived at Prospect Station.

Bright and early next morning, the 8th, we and the sun arose together, and both set out for a day's journey to the west. It was General Sheridan's impression that the enemy's movement across the Appomattox at Farmville was a blind, intended to baffle and mislead pursuit; he knew that as he had abandoned Danville as a base of supplies he would have to find another, and Lynchburg was the only depot that offered, so he concluded that sooner or later his advance would appear on the Lynchburg Road, and then the general proposed to be in the neighborhood. Our line of march to-day was therefore parallel to the railroad, and the general determined that the main column should not be diverted by any side issues or any reports of Lee's meanderings beyond the Appomattox. Just before mounting his horse, he wrote to the lieutenant-general to let him know that the troopers were in the saddle, and to drop one of his urgent spurs upon the flank of the main army of pursuit. He said: "I will move on Appomattox Court House. Should we not intercept the enemy, and he be forced into Lynchburg, surrender there is beyond question." Appomattox Court House is on the Richmond and Lynchburg Pike, commonly called the Cumberland Road, five miles to the north and east of Appomattox Station, where the pike crosses the Lynchburg Railroad, and on the Cumberland Road Lee was reported to be marching. From this dispatch, then, we glean the general's intentions, and learn that Appomattox Court House, to be so famous in history, did not blunder into notoriety, but came by it through deep design. Our programme of the day was very simple. We would march rapidly to Appomattox depot, and if Lee had ordered supplies to await him there, would receipt for them in his name; if no force of the enemy had yet reached the station, we would turn to the right, on the Cumberland Road, and go as far as the Court House to meet them. This would be civil and at the same time serve the interest of both parties, for there was no use in any more fighting, and if we could block the road at the Court House while General Meade followed Lee's rear, there would be an end of it.

From the woods about Prospect Station (at which point we found neither station nor prospect), the cavalry was pouring out as we rode up with the general; Merritt led off, with Custer in advance, followed by Devin, and Crook brought up the rear—MacKenzie, having left us to report again to General Ord, was not of our party to-day. As the general gained the head of the column, a short distance beyond the station, one of Young's scouts met us and reported that already there were four trains of cars at Appomattox depot awaiting General Lee.

The general heard this joyfully. His dead-reckoning was verified now by the scout who had had an observation, and he could press on confidently to harbor; so passing the word to Merritt and Crook to shake out the last reef and carry all sail, he set his eyes on the distant horizon and bore down for Appomattox depot, twenty-five miles away.

The roads were not so bad as usual, the soil being somewhat sandy, and we made capital time, halting only once, for rest and water. The general took advantage of this waiting place to send a regiment off to the right to Cutbank Ford, near the head-waters of the Appomattox, to see if any of the enemy were coming across to our side; but all was reported quiet there, and the river was flowing on undisturbed. It was a day of uneventful marching, and we hardly saw a human being all the way; the country had never been withered by war's touch, and the fields had been peacefully plowed for the coming crops; fences were up, and the woods had all their growth; the sparse farm-houses seemed to be inhabited, and the farms to be tilled by ample contrabands. If it was not the garden-spot of the world, as tradition might have led us to expect, it was a home of rude plenty and peace until now; and the weather being fine and our spirits good, the ride was a very enjoyable one. When the sun was only an hour high in the west, energetic Custer, in advance, spied the depot and four heavy trains of freight cars lying there innocently, with the white smoke of the locomotives curling over the trees; he quickly ordered his leading regiments to circle out to the left through the woods, and then, as they gained the railroad beyond the station and galloped down upon the astonished engineers and collared them before they could mount their iron horses, he led the rest of his division pell-mell down the road, and enveloped the trains as quick as winking. Custer might not well conduct a siege of regular approaches; but for a sudden dash, Custer against the world. Many another might have pricked his fingers badly with meddling gently with this nettle, but he took it in his hand boldly and crushed it: for it was a nettle, and a very keen one, as appeared in a moment when there opened on his slap-dash party a banging of batteries going off like a bunch of fire-crackers. Custer was a good deal struck aback but not upset. He kept his wits about him enough to man the trains and start them off toward Farmville for safe keeping, and they were puffing up the road as General Sheridan, in the midst of Custer's galloping division, reached the station. Then he turned his attention to the guns, and dashed into the woods to see who was firing so wildly, and to see if it couldn't be stopped. General Sheridan rode rapidly to the right to look at the ground, and sent word to Merritt to bring Devin up there at a trot, and put him to work in the enemy's rear, and then returned to Custer, who, concluding that there was more sound than force in the woods, was going in to silence the one and bag the other. Devin, under Merritt's directions, took a wood-path to the right, and soon found a fine open field, dipping gently to a broad valley, and rising again beyond to the ridge of a commanding hill, from whose top the last gleams of sunset were just ricochetting into the air. Dismounting his men as they came into line, he moved down into the valley, where a marsh bothered him some, and then bearing to his left, went into the woods on the hillside. He was a little slow for the crisis, but no harm came of it, for Custer had meanwhile scoured about in his random way, recklessly riding down all opposers, and, the force with the guns proving more noisy than numerous, he had captured nearly all of both before Devin opened his fire. Then they pushed on together, mounted and dismounted, driving before them, toward Appomattox Court House, the surprised and demoralized enemy.

These guns and troops had not come to the depot with any expectation of finding a fight there; they were only the advance of Lee's column on the Cumberland Road, and fighting was far from their thoughts. A feed was what they were after, and even the guns must have smacked their lips sympathetically as they went into park in sight of the trains of supplies; so when Custer rudely snatched away the meal, the hungry gunners, who had so fiercely resisted his theft, had no stomach for a fight in lieu of a supper, and losing one against their will, had no inclination for the other. Therefore they surrendered, for the most part, as the cavalry charged them from every side, and a thousand or more of them took the chances of supper with us.

By the time that Devin had joined Custer it was quite dark, and, no serious opposition occurring, they halted for the night in the woods, a mile or two on the road to the Court House; and after becoming satisfied that the fighting for the night was over, the general sent the following dispatch rapidly to General Grant, who was marching with General Meade on the other side of the Appomattox:

> Cavalry Headquarters,
> Appomattox Station,
> *April 8th*, 1865.
>
> Lieut.-General U. S. Grant,
> *Commanding Armies United States:*
>
> General—We have captured four trains of cars with locomotives, twenty-five pieces of ar-

tillery, and a large number of wagons and prisoners. The trains, one of which was burned, were loaded with supplies.

If it is possible to push on your troops we may have handsome results in the morning.

(Signed)   P. H. SHERIDAN,
Major-General.

Then retiring to a little house near the depot, and stretching out on a bench in the cheerful parlor, which a bright wood fire comfortably furnished otherwise, he immediately dictated the following:

CAVALRY HEADQUARTERS,
April 8th, 1865,
9.20 P.M.

LIEUT.-GENERAL U. S. GRANT,
Commanding Armies United States:

GENERAL—I marched early this morning from Buffalo Creek and Prospect Station on Appomattox depot, where my scouts had reported trains of cars with supplies for Lee's army. A short time before dusk General Custer, who had the advance, made a dash at the station, capturing four trains of supplies with locomotives. One of the trains was burned, and the others run by him toward Farmville for security. Custer then pushed on toward Appomattox Court House, driving the enemy, who kept up a heavy fire of artillery, charging them repeatedly, and capturing, as far as reported, twenty-five pieces of artillery, and a number of prisoners and wagons. The first cavalry division supported him on the right.

A reconnoissance sent across the Appomattox reports the enemy moving on the Cumberland Road to Appomattox Station, where they expected to get supplies.

Custer is still pushing on. If General Gibbon and the Fifth Corps can get up to-night we will perhaps finish the job in the morning. I do not think Lee means to surrender until compelled to do so.

(Signed)   P. H. SHERIDAN,
Major-General.

As Lee was compelled to surrender next morning, this is the last dispatch which the general found it necessary to write. All through the campaign he had been urging on the whole army by word and example, and now he was to see his hopes realized, his confidence vindicated, and his labor repaid. From the morning that we saw him riding out of his camp below Petersburg until this hour, he had never doubted for a moment that a crowning victory would attend our arms should the whole force be put vigorously in and opening success thoroughly followed up. Looking back over what he wrote to the lieutenant-general, we may see how from the first he did not hesitate to commit himself to the defeat and capture of Lee, and how he boldly avowed his belief in entire success, shouldering, as it were, the responsibility of the undertaking, and rendering himself liable to the severest criticism if failure had ensued. As early as the 31st of March, in the mud at Dinwiddie Court House, he wrote: "If the ground would permit, I believe I could, with the Sixth Corps, turn the enemy's left flank (at Five Forks) or cut up their lines;" and we have seen how he made good this declaration with the Fifth Corps the next day, and when this was done how he promptly moved against the flank of Lee's main line at Petersburg, without waiting for orders. From the Namozine Road, on the 4th of April, two days before the decisive battle of Sailor's Creek, he wrote: "If we press on we will no doubt get the whole army." At Jetersville, the next afternoon, he said in his dispatch: "I wish you were here yourself. I feel confident of capturing the Army of Northern Virginia if we exert ourselves. I see no escape for Lee." Then, as the enemy staggered back from the blow he dealt them at Sailor's Creek, he wrote: "If the thing is pressed, I think that Lee will surrender." And at sunrise and dark to-day he had three times renewed these confident and urgent messages: "I will move on Appomattox Court House. Should we not intercept the enemy, and he be forced into Lynchburg, surrender there is beyond question." "If it is possible to push on your troops, we may have handsome results in the morning." "If General Gibbon and the Fifth Corps can get up to-night we will perhaps finish the job in the morning. I do not think Lee means to surrender until compelled to do so."

Truly he stands deep to-night in pledges for success, and if victory attend us in the morning, his share of the joy and glory will have been richly deserved.

CHAPTER VIII.

THE NINTH OF APRIL, SIXTY-FIVE.

THE troops of General Gibbon and the Fifth Corps, to which General Sheridan alludes in his last dispatch, were those which General Grant had sent down to Prince Edward Court House from Farmville to follow the trail of the cavalry; they had pressed on vigorously after us, and had now responded to General Sheridan's appeal of last evening for one final effort, by marching all night long, and the head of their column was pattering by our headquarters before daylight on the morning of the ninth. Although General Sheridan knew very well that the remnant of Lee's army confronted him on the road to Appomattox Court House, and would try to break through to the railroad at sunrise, he never thought of abandoning his position there even if the infantry could not get up. If at daylight he should have to bear the brunt of Lee's attack alone, he would impede him as much as he could and make slow marching for him till support could come to the relief of the cavalry, which now, knowing nothing of the reinforcement that was so near at hand, was preparing to mount to be ready for the shock.

With the advance of the infantry column came General Ord, of the Army of the James, who was General Sheridan's superior officer, and therefore would control the infantry troops; so after a short consultation with him, the general started on to look after the cavalrymen, who by this time were skirmishing briskly with the advancing enemy. Crook was in advance and soon was hotly engaged; dismounting his men and rapidly running his guns to the front, he resisted their heavy onset with determined pluck, holding on to his ground with a grip which at first the enemy found it hard to loose; but their force was infantry, fighting for a point that must be gained or all would be lost, and they greatly outnumbered Crook's division. On the day before, General Lee had written to General Grant: "To be frank, I do not consider that the emergency has arisen to call for the surrender of this army;" and if it had not arisen, it was only because of the open road to Danville. If that were closed, then a faint glimmer of necessity to entertain surrender would probably break upon General Lee, so doubtless he got up this morning prepared to prove that the emergency which he had repudiated did not exist; and as he had no time to trifle, he came down to this doorway prepared to accept a peaceful passage, or to batter his way through if opposed. Evidently his men were aware of how much depended on forcing an exit, and as they came across lots from the

Court House, they didn't stop to note the springing grass, nor step aside from the tender flowers just opening in their path, but pressed on with ruthless tramp, and scared the pleasant Sunday with their fierce volleys and slap-banging of heavy guns. As the chimes of the early church-bells at home pealed their sweet matins, which clashed harmoniously in mid-air like cymbals, these fields trembled under the sounding peals of war's clangor, which met discordantly and were hurled in gruff rumblings far over the hills.

For a little while Crook stood his ground; but when General Sheridan came up and looked about him, he sent back word to Generals Ord and Griffin to hurry on, and ordered Crook to fall back slowly and not sacrifice his men by trying to check the heavy force attacking him. The enemy's line was not moving down the road but was formed almost parallel to it, and on the left as they looked toward the depot. To confront them, then, our infantry, which had marched up the road, faced to the right and moved into the woods, in whose front Crook's command was fighting. Merritt was ordered, now, to get his divisions mounted and move round the right of our infantry line, and Crook, as he retired, was instructed to give way in the same direction, in order to leave a fair field in front. Gibbon with the Twenty-fourth Corps, Griffin with the Fifth, and a division of colored troops belonging to General Ord's command, were now ensconced among the trees silently waiting for orders to advance. On the extreme left General Davies was skirmishing with some rebel cavalry, and MacKenzie was out there, somewhere, stealing round to their flank. Apparently we were deserting the field; our cavalry had almost ceased to resist the enemy's advance, and from sharp and close fighting (so close that one of Crook's batteries lost a gun), they had gradually relapsed into a passive condition, as if they accepted the situation and would now permit General Lee to pass on unmolested.

Seeing our troopers march off by the flank, apparently giving up the fight for the road and opening a way of retreat, Lee's men yelled and quickened their pace and doubled their fire; they would get away after all, they thought, for Sheridan's cavalry alone couldn't hope to stop them, and evidently we had no other troops at hand. Appomattox depot gained, their troubles would be at an end, for thence the road to Danville is straight; at last they would have cast us behind them and we might catch them if we could. Fast walkers they and not much encumbered with *impedimenta*, they could laugh at our heavily-loaded infantry if once they could shake it from the flank; and if ever they should join Johnston—well, wonderful things would happen then, so they gave us their best yell and pressed on faster. But not far. For the sound of their peculiar cheer had hardly entered the woods, before the long lines of our infantry emerged and burst upon their astonished sight. They staggered back as Don Giovanni does before the ghost, and their whole line wavered as if each particular man was terror-struck like Leporello. They didn't even fire, palsied as they were by surprise, but rolled back like a receding wave which has spent the force of its assault against the earth-works of the shore.

Then our troops advanced, quietly and grimly, saving their cheers for the end of the rebellion, which everybody felt must soon be reached. The undulating lines of the infantry, now rising the crest of a knoll, now dipping into a valley or ravine, pressed on grandly across the open; for here at last we were out of the woods in the beautiful clear fields stretching away to the horizon, and here, if the rebellion should crumble, all who fought against it might see its fall. The cavalry on the right trotted out in advance of the infantry line, and made ready to take the enemy in flank if he should stand to fight, or dash at his trains, which were now in full view beyond Appomattox Court House. At the head of the horsemen rode Custer, of the golden locks, his broad sombrero turned up from his hard, bronzed face, the ends of his crimson cravat floating over his shoulders, gold galore spangling his jacket sleeves, a pistol in his boot, jangling spurs on his heels, and a ponderous claymore swinging at his side,—a wild, dare-devil of a general, and a prince of advance-guards, quick to see and act. Seeing him pass by, a stranger might smile and say "Who's that?" as he noticed his motley wear, his curls, and his quick, impetuous way, but would wonder to see him in the thick of a fight; for Custer loves fighting, and hated his enemies then.

As he is about to strike a final blow for the good cause, his hand is stayed and his great sword drops back again into the scabbard, for out from the enemy's lines comes a rider, "bound on bound," bearing a white flag of truce, to ask for time to consummate surrender. General Sheridan is just behind, and word is sent to him at once, though the wild cheers of the men have passed the good news back on the wind, and he meets the messenger half way. The general notifies General Ord, and the whole line is halted on the crest overlooking Appomattox Court House and the valley beyond, in which lies broken the Army of Northern Virginia. As we gain the crest, there is no organized line of the enemy visible below, though their skirmishers, which are halted on the farther side of the Court House, confront ours on this side, man for man. Behind them is a mass of men and matter unavailable for fighting. Groups of soldiers are sitting about or wandering off to the wagon trains, which stand huddled together in disorderly park, with batteries which seem tangled up badly, some facing one way and some another, as if divided in opinion whether to advance or retreat. There is nothing worthy the name of an army, and nothing that looks competent to uphold the Confederacy for another half hour. As word is passed along our line to halt, the truth breaks on the men, and rousing cheers follow the orders from right to left.

General Sheridan, confiding in the flag of truce, and trusting to a complete cessation of hostilities as a matter of course, rode out in front of his cavalry and struck across toward Appomattox Court House, which was about the center of the position our troops held at halting. But his faith proved to be ill-founded, for he had hardly gone a hundred yards when some rebel troops in front of him suddenly fired on his little party. Luckily they aimed badly, and nobody was hurt, and the general and his staff, supposing some mistake was at the bottom of this eccentric proceeding, waved their caps, and made other friendly signals, only to be answered by another volley, happily as ineffectual as the first; then, galloping away, they found shelter behind a hill, while the officer who had brought the flag of truce, and Major Allen, of our staff, rode rapidly into the enemy's lines, on the flank of this dangerous party, and demanded to know the cause of this violation of the flag. A general in command, who evidently supposed himself to be General Taylor in Mexico, replied that South

Carolinians never surrendered, and declined to receive any order to suspend hostilities. He was doubtless seeking to die in the last ditch, and the opportunity was likely to be soon afforded him, for Custer, hearing this firing in the direction the general had taken, promptly moved out to look into it.

Meanwhile the general wended his way more carefully to the Court House, and there was met by the Confederate generals Gordon and Wilcox on the neutral ground between the picket-lines, in the midst of which Appomattox Court House happened to stand. Just as they began to talk, firing was heard again on our right where the contumacious South Carolinians were. General Gordon looked up anxiously, and ordered a staff officer to go rapidly and find out what it meant, but General Sheridan said: "Never mind! never mind! I know what it is. Let them fight it out!" and then explained that the bold general who never surrendered had fallen into the hands of Custer, and was likely to come to terms or grief very shortly. In a moment all was quiet again, and the last angry shot had been fired from the war-worn lines, which now could only stack arms, sling carbines, return sabers, and await the result of the negotiations for surrender.

General Gordon asked for a suspension of hostilities, and said that General Lee was prepared to surrender his army, and would immediately send to General Grant a communication to that effect. General Sheridan replied that he was very anxious to avoid further loss of life, but the effort of the morning hadn't looked like an intention to surrender, and he must have some certain assurance that this was a bona fide proposition, and not a make-shift to gain time and advantage. Both General Gordon and General Wilcox earnestly declared their entire good faith, and said Lee's case was hopeless now, and he must surrender and would. There could be no doubt of their sincerity or of the pass to which Lee had come, and so General Sheridan agreed to wait for further developments, and returned to our lines, promising to meet these officers again at the Court House in half an hour.

Meanwhile General Ord came up, and others began to gather from right to left; but there was no excitement at all. After the first cheer, the tired troops had stretched themselves on the ground at full length, and were calmly surveying the novel scene of a harmless enemy in front. Indians couldn't have conducted themselves with more propriety, or have observed a more serene indifference in the face of a matter of surpassing interest; and a stranger arriving on the ground would have said the halt was only a rest, that nothing unusual had occurred, and that the march would be resumed after coffee. As the generals rode up there was some hand-shaking, more smiles than are often seen in line of battle, but nobody was very demonstrative. If we believe that men of rough natures have underlying them some finer sensibilities which do not openly find expression, let us say that all this quiet was the index of a feeling of overpowering gratitude to Heaven that on this Sabbath day they were permitted to see the sun shining on the downfall of rebellion, and gilding the hope of country restored, friends reunited, and enemies disarmed.

When the half hour was up, General Ord and General Sheridan, together with several other officers of rank, rode through the pickets again, and met the Confederate generals at the Court House. General Longstreet was there this time —a grisly-looking man, disabled in one arm, and bearing all over the evidences of hard campaigns and traces of disappointment in his troubled face—and he bore a dispatch from Lee to General Grant. It was in answer to one that the lieutenant-general had sent to him stating the terms on which he would receive his surrender, and was in these words:

April 9th, 1865.

LIEUTENANT-GENERAL U. S. GRANT:

GENERAL—I received your note of this morning on the picket-line, whither I had come to meet you and ascertain definitely what terms were embraced in your proposal of yesterday with reference to the surrender of this army. I now ask an interview, in accordance with the offer contained in your letter of yesterday, for that purpose.

(Signed) R. E. LEE,
General.

With this dispatch General Sheridan immediately sent off a staff officer to find General Grant, who was reported to be on his way from General Meade to Appomattox Court House. Taking a wood-road leading off in the direction from which the lieutenant-general would come, the officer rode fast on his errand, and after galloping some five or six miles and striking the main road on which we had marched the day before, fortunately met General Grant just beyond the intersection, rapidly pacing down this road in search of General Sheridan. Turning off into the woods at a lively trot, the party was not long in reaching the Court House (and would have gained it sooner but for stupidly missing the way and almost wandering into Lee's lines), and there it was found that the second interview had not been much longer than the first, and that all of our officers had come back inside the pickets. As General Grant rode up, Generals Ord and Sheridan and the rest were standing on foot at the end of the broad grassy street which intersects the Court House—that is, the town. The lieutenant-general dismounted, came forward, and said: "How are you, Sheridan?"

To which, in a piert manner, the general replied: "First rate, thank you; how are you?"

"Is General Lee up there?"

"Yes."

"Well, then, we'll go up."

This is all that was said at that time, and the conversation, in view of all the circumstances, would illustrate a statement that we are not a very demonstrative or dramatic people. In effective groupings and treatment of remarkable occasions the people of the other continent can give us heavy odds. How poor this seems by the side of the Prussian king and Bismarck hunting over the field of Sadowa for the Crown Prince, whom, when found, the king grapples to his soul, decorates his manly bosom with beautiful insignia of honor and glory; and then their feelings master them, and king and prince and Bismarck (Heaven save the marck!) burst out crying, field and staff officers joining in. And yet our field of Appomattox Court House was more than the field of Sadowa. What recollections had they there of years of alternate disaster and victory; what memories of hard campaigns and well-contested fields; of friendship cemented by the trials of camp and battle; of patient watching and anxious thought; of the fierce attack and the stubborn defense; of waiting, and work, and war? If they had had any such, thronging into their minds, and had met on the evening of Sadowa, as our generals met now, it is painful to contemplate what they might have done. The king would probably have stood upon his head; Bismarck would have nimbly climbed to his upturned feet; to him the Crown Prince would have vaulted through the air, and from this perilous height would have made a leap to astonish the Buislay brothers, while the Count, flying out with extended arms, would have caught him descending, as Young America catches the swinging trapeze; and the king would have died dramatically of a rush of blood to the brain. But we don't understand that sort of thing, and the result is what we have cited.

So Generals Grant, Ord, and Sheridan, with three or four staff officers each, went up to the Court House, and of our staff there went three, a senior aide, the chief of staff, and the adjutant-general. The town consists of about five houses, a tavern, and a court house, all on one street, and that was boarded up at one end to keep the cows out. On the right hand side as we went in was the principal residence, owned by Mr. McLean, and to his house General Grant was conducted to meet General Lee. At the fence the whole party dismounted, and walking over a narrow grass-plot to the house noticed General Lee's gray horse nibbling there in charge of an orderly, who was holding his own as well. General Grant entered the house with one or two of his staff, and the rest of us sat down on the piazza and waited. Mr. McLean was out there, too, but was so much excited by his appreciation of passing events that he didn't know where his pump was, or if he had any, and if not, couldn't tell us where there was a spring. In a moment Colonel Babcock came out, smiling, whirled his hat round his head once, and beckoned Generals Ord and Sheridan to come in. They walked the floor silently, as people do who have first peep at a baby, and after awhile General Lee came out and signaled to his orderly to bridle his horse. While this was being done, he stood on the lowest step of the piazza (we had all risen respectfully as he passed down), and looking over into the valley toward his army, smote his hands together several times in an absent sort of way, utterly unconscious of the people about him, and seeming to see nothing till his horse was led in front of him. As he stood there he appeared to be about sixty years of age, a tall, soldierly figure of a man, with a full gray beard, a new suit of gray clothes, a high gray felt hat, with a cord, long buckskin gauntlets, high riding boots, and a beautiful sword. He was all that our fancy had painted him; and he had the sympathy of us all as he rode away. Just as he gathered up his bridle, General Grant went down the steps, and, passing in front of his horse, touched his hat to General Lee, who made a similar salute, and then left the yard and returned to his own lines with his orderly and the single staff officer who had accompanied him to the interview, and who was said to have been Colonel Marshall, his chief of staff, a quiet-looking man, in spectacles, looking more like one of thought than of action. General Grant presented something of a contrast to General Lee in the way of uniform, not only in color, but in style and general effect. He had on a sugar-loaf hat, almost peculiar to himself, a frock coat, unbuttoned and splashed with mud, a dark vest, dark-blue pantaloons tucked into top-boots, muddy also, and no sword. His countenance wasn't relaxed at all, and not a muscle of his face told tales on his thoughts. If he was very much pleased by the surrender of Lee, nothing in his air or manner indicated it. The joyful occasion didn't seem to awaken in him a responsive echo, and he went and mounted his horse and rode away silently, to send off a dispatch which should electrify the North and set all the church-bells ringing jubilant vespers on this happy Sunday evening.

As soon as he had gone, the officers sitting about the porch suddenly bethought them to secure relics of this event by carrying away the greater portion of the house in which it happened. The most important and valuable, of course, were the materials and articles of furniture that had been used to draw up and sign Lee's letter of surrender; and these were scuffled for manfully, and the quickest bore off the prize. The brawny Custer might have been seen proudly marching away with the table on his shoulders at which Lee sat, the rest crying out "Sheridan's

Robbers" as he went off; but they didn't know that General Sheridan had bought it of Mr. McLean for twenty dollars in specie (the general being injudiciously long in gold at this crisis), and had sent it to Mrs. Custer with his compliments. The moral guard which had kept away the crowd during the presence of the lieutenant-general was now relieved, and curious officers of every grade inundated the house. Everything that would do for a relic, however unwieldy, was confiscated or bought, and Mr. McLean seemed likely to pay a high price for the glory of going down to history on the arm of a great event. Somebody suddenly thought of the pen. Where was that? That was the thing for his money: and this suggestion was followed by another burst of relic-hunters, who threatened to overturn the principal officers of the army in their effort to profit by it. Probably this was the last relic that anybody would think of, everything else having been gleaned; so to get rid of the mob, and for the sake of peace and quiet, now that the war was over, a staff officer, who had been at the house during the ceremonies of surrender, drew from his pocket a gold case-pen, and holding it aloft declared that General Lee had borrowed it of him to sign his name to the letter of capitulation; and this declaration, which turned out to be an infamous lie, evoked many congratulations and much envy. But it had the effect to break the ranks of the relic-hunters, who slowly dispersed to their several commands; and then those who had not cared to run amuck for chairs and table-legs, clipped a budding flower from the bushes in the garden and sent it home as an emblem of peace, with thankful hearts.

Meanwhile there was a great stir in General Lee's army, and they were still cheering wildly as we left McLean's house to find a camp for ourselves. Of course his intention to surrender had been noised abroad, and as he returned from his interview with General Grant he was greeted with the applause we were now hearing. Cheer after cheer marked his progress through the old ranks that had supported him so gallantly; but what or why they were cheering seems not to be fully decided. The Southern writers of the day agreed that they applauded General Lee thus to show for him their sympathy in his misfortunes and their devotion to him and the lost cause. The latter reason is possible, but the former is not probable; sympathy for sorrow and calamity does not find such loud expression in crowds any more than it does in individuals. Nobody would give three cheers for a man who had lost his father, with the idea of soothing him. When Queen Victoria made her first public appearance in England, after the death of the Prince Consort, it was reported that as her carriage moved down the Strand, the thousands who had gathered there to welcome her suppressed the rising cheer and stood all silent with one consent as she passed by; and will anybody say that the army of the Confederacy was less sympathetic than an English crowd, and less keenly alive to a proper regard for misfortune? Doubtless Lee's army was sorry for him, because his loss was theirs, and when his hope foundered theirs went down, too; but it was not because of his loss that they cheered so long and loud. It was because he had surrendered; because he had confessed defeat at last, though all they had known he was defeated long before; because they saw in surrender some hope of beginning life anew to repair the blunder of the Confederacy; and, thanking him for this, the brave fellows who stood by him to the last, and would have died rather than desert the cause, cheered him rapturously as he returned to tell them that they were set at liberty.

In the evening we sent rations for 20,000 men into his hungry camp, and he released our hungry prisoners, who came joyfully into our lines, with Irvine Gregg at the head of them, serene as usual, but with a good appetite. Then we went to bed, and had a good night's rest, and tried to appreciate the great blessing of peace that had suddenly descended upon us.

CHAPTER IX.

BREAKING RANKS.

THEN there was the slow march back to Petersburg, saddened by the news we got at Nottoway Court House of the death of President Lincoln. We had a tent pitched in our camp there for a telegraph operator of our own, who, at ten o'clock on the night after the assassination, came running to the general with an incoherent dispatch which he said he had copied from a message that had passed by on the wires to General Meade's headquarters at Burkesville, farther up the Southside Railroad. It was signed by Major Eckert of the War Department, and reported that President Lincoln had been shot at Willard's Hotel at ten o'clock that morning and would certainly die. None of us believed it. We asked each other what would the President be doing at Willard's Hotel at ten o'clock in the morning. It was a hoax, evidently. It was so badly expressed, too,—the words all jumbled together in a way that no officer of the War Department would send an important message. The general read it without the least visible emotion and passed it to one of his staff, who whistled incredulously and passed it on. After inspection it was universally condemned; we were not to be sold by a telegraph operator, drunk, probably, and trying to get up an excitement in the army. If the story was true, why didn't the Secretary of War notify the army? Who the deuce is "T. T. Eckert, Major, etc."? every one asked. May be everybody but the major was shot, somebody said. In fact it was so shocking, *if* true, that by common consent it was only to be ridiculed; and so we went to bed, offering to bet anything that there wasn't a word of truth in it.

How this distorted dispatch was ever telegraphed was not explained, but next morning we had official information of the President's death which left no room for doubt, and the joy of the army was turned into mourning; men who could laugh at disaster in the field and hope for better luck next time, who could cook coffee five minutes after recrossing the river from Fredericksburg, and forget all about the heights of St. Marye in Killikinnick, had sad faces now, for the army was as keenly alive to the President's character as the people, and realized how necessary such a character is to the safe conduct of affairs through the delicate diplomacy which the new situation demanded. The most hopeful predicted trouble ahead for the new *régime;* and if trouble shall come in an unexpected way, it will be trouble none the less, and the foreboding none the less fulfilled, and the honest President none the less worthily mourned.

After a short rest at Petersburg there was the pic-nic-ing excursion toward Danville, North Carolina, to assist in the campaign against Johnston in case of his demanding to be conquered on his own account instead of falling with the downfall of Lee, as he wisely and honorably concluded to do; and then there was the long return to Washington, where we dissolved the great co-partnership. But our headquarters — traveling partners in the firm — couldn't wait for the formal dissolution. The silent partner sent us off to Texas to look after Kirby Smith, and we had to say good-by to the rest in a hurry and leave behind us the coming glories of the Grand Review; which was a disappointment, and we may as well own it. Of course we had the high and mighty military idea of duty to be done; considered that of late we had done no more than the Union expects every man to do, and had the proper indifference to popular applause, and all that; yet it may be now confessed that, from the general to his orderly, there was a suspicion of regret pervading this patriotic party, that we were not to ride up Pennsylvania Avenue at the head of "Sheridan's cavalry," and be welcomed by the "thundering cheer of the street."

However, a sense of martyrdom is perhaps almost as agreeable as applause, and we consoled ourselves with the thought how dulce and decorum it is to be sacrificed pro patria, and had quite recovered a becoming frame of mind by the time our train had started.

Here at Washington, though, the campaign ends when we shake hands with the old cavalry party and propose their jolly good healths at our last lunch at Willard's. At odd times on the road, we have been associated with sundry other gallant commanders and various gallant troops; but they all have returned to their respective places, and now only with cavalrymen do we feel that we sever a tie at parting. It is to them that we fill now—to Merritt, who has done so much good fighting and won so little printed fame, a man of brains, with a boyish face and a splendid head; to Custer, quick as a flash, daring and reckless almost without equal, yet showing coolness and judgment in some tight places; to Devin, who is of the school of Polonius, a little slow sometimes in entrance to a fight, but being in, as slow to leave a point for which the enemy is trying; who cut off his beard because it was growing gray, declaring the rôle of "old Devin" to be played out, and won his stars forthwith by the virtue of a smooth chin; to Gibbes, courteous, jolly, and hospitable, always ready with his brigade for whatever fortune found for him to do; to Irvine Gregg, "cool as a clock," looking out from under his broad slouch-hat on any phase of battle; to Smith, of Maine, steady as a light-house and to be counted on in an awkward pinch, sturdy in form and character, and looking like Governor Carver, the Puritan, leaning on his sword at the landing at Plymouth Rock; to Crook, easy going and kindly, who has done more good service than has been blown to his credit through "the trumpet that speaks of fame;" to Davies, earnest and dashing, always getting horses killed and balls through his boots, a strict disciplinarian and efficient in camp and field; to Fitzhugh, who left his battery to command a brigade, and more than sustained his old reputation; to all the rest unnamed who have fought with the troopers in this campaign; to the old associations with D. McM. Gregg, Torbert, Wilson, McIntosh and the others, who in earlier campaigns were prominent in Sheridan's cavalry and made it famous by their swords; and to the glorious memory of those who have fallen.

Then to the chief, with all the honors. He has done much to make the cavalry illustrious, and his name is linked with it everywhere. "Sheridan's cavalry" is now the Alma Mater of the horsemen, and the Head-Center of the best *esprit de corps*. There is a good deal of regimental pride, of course, and the honor of his brigade and division is something to every man; but ask a trooper in a general way to what he belongs, and he will begin with "Sheridan's cavalry," and take you down the successive steps to his regiment afterward in case you want to go. It is like the (North) American's answer that he belongs to "the States" when you meet him abroad and ask him his home; he is nothing loth to tell you his State and city and dilate on their beauties at length if you like, but he feels that his chief glory is in the Republic, and fancies that the effulgence of its institutions beams from him, as a representative. And, like the States, Sheridan's cavalry is a cloak that covers good and bad alike, and the distinction which is sufficient for the best men in the best regiments in the command, is a brilliant covering to some whose single worth would perhaps have earned but poor renown. Such share of the glory of this title as properly belongs to the general all are ready to award; nowhere in the army are more harmonious relations and mutual respect, and nowhere would a parting be more keenly felt.

In taking leave of him let us simply accord to him the credit which history will give to his rare ability and soldierly qualities. With the material which he found ready to his hand (and certainly it would be hard to find better) he established at the outset a good understanding, and, never proving captious or unfair, retained the confidence of all and obtained results which, without hearty co-operation and good-will, could never have been recorded, developing meanwhile a genius of his own which in some special phases has been unequaled in the war. Speaking of him as we have seen him in this campaign, if others were wanting, may we not ascribe to him a rare combination of military power: prudence and judgment to plan; energy and courage to execute; dash and vigor to follow up advantage; unbounded faith to "attempt the end, and never stand to doubt;" and, withal, ability to cope with sudden emergencies, and patience to defend when assault is turned upon him? As the gallant leader of the cavalry advance to-day, as the brilliant general handling an army in its support to-morrow, where shall we find greater or more varied ability? If we grant him only the specialty which this campaign has illustrated, where could we have looked for one to take his place? The army does not contain his counterpart, and, if he had fallen, there would have been

> "Sighing that nature formed but one such man,
> And broke the die in moulding Sheridan."

So much it is right to say of him, for it is the truth, and though more might be said perhaps, with equal truth, of his ability in other spheres, it is not worth while to go further than the scope of this narration, lest some one think we are idealizing him, which at the outset we promised not to do. In fact it is not worth while to idealize anybody nowadays, for we don't set up an image of a living hero said to be done in gold, and stand far off and worship it; but in this enlightened country we go very near to whatever is put before the public, and scratch the surface ruthlessly to learn its true worth, and if it isn't the real thing it gets knocked off the pedestal of public favor sooner or later. So it is idle to set up false claims in a man's behalf and gain for him a short life of popular belief in them, and a sudden fall from honor when the claims are disallowed; therefore, temperate praise has been studied in this slender narrative, lest any one should say that fancy outweighs fact.

And now that the reader may know General Sheridan if he meet him, and not complain that friendship has disguised him past recognition, let us take a parting look at him across the table as we drink his health, and long life to him, and a pretty wife.

He has not seen more than five and thirty summers, and is not tall of his years, but, as his brain is not cramped by his inches, nobody has ever lost confidence in him on that account; for

> "Though not a Giant, he is learned and wise,
> And wisdom compensates for want of size."

His mental stature is not easily measured, and men whose eyes look over his head are puzzled to know how much is in it. His military caliber, too, is hard to guess, and he would be a clever soldier who could claim to have found it out; he has been competent for every emergency that he has been called upon to meet, and for the largest command he ever controlled, but nobody is found to say what emergency would stagger him, or what number of troops would prove too many for him.

His face is flushed, not with wine, but with life, and his eyes twinkle like stars; the ends of his moustache curl up with decision, and his *mouche* hides the sharp outline of his chin; his uniform coat is buttoned to the throat, across a square deep chest, which rightly indicates his physical power, and he is very simply dressed throughout, with nothing of the gay cavalier about him. He talks slowly and very quietly, smiling now, and working his mouth cross-wise. If excited on the field, he won't bluster, but *may* swear, and be not so careful of the elegancies of speech as are some *dilettanti* people, who never have many thoughts of their own to express and never mingle in stirring events; one of whom,

> "That never set a squadron in the field,
> Nor the division of a battle knows,"

might perhaps be shocked in these fiery moments, but if he has a chance for a quiet chat with the general, will think him rather gentle than otherwise, and begin to doubt the terrible oaths and fierce imprecations of song and story; will find him proud of the achievements of his various commands, but modest about his own performances, and as silent as a pyramid if a speech is to be made. Accustomed to reserve, and not having the faculty of hiding himself in words, he resorts to the unusual expedient of silence, and the public never would have known him but for the great events which called him out. With them he can grapple, but a serenading party is too much for him. If the reader has occasion to correspond with him, any of his staff will be happy to decipher his hasty reply, and assure the correspondent that the signature is not copied from the Rosetta stone, but is the sign-manual of "yours truly, P. H. Sheridan, Major-General."

So much for the generals who have won glory and renown.

But before we rise from this festivity, let us join in remembering "the boys," who deserve a bumper filled to the beaker's brim.

> "Pledge me round. I bid ye declare,
> All good fellows whose beards are gray,"

and otherwise:

Have they not followed the Flag unfalteringly, though they lost many comrades by the way, who gave their lives unsparingly to fill the chasm that was dividing the Union? Let us cherish the memory of these; and the blessings they have secured by such unstinted sacrifice let us not forfeit now,

"Ere yet ever a month is gone."

THE END

www.ingramcontent.com/pod-product-compliance
Lightning Source LLC
Chambersburg PA
CBHW021816230426
43669CB00008B/770